D1535505

FLORIDA STATE
UNIVERSITY LIBRARIES

MAY 14 1990

TALLAHASSEE, FLORIDA

# INTEREST RATE VOLATILITY

Understanding, Analyzing, and Managing Interest Rate Risk and Risk-Based Capital

# HOW CAN WE HELP YOU???

**Thank you** for your interest in this product. *Irwin Professional* is the leading publisher of trade and professional information for sophisticated individuals and business, investment and financial professionals.

From its inception in 1965, and through the recent acquisition of Probus Publishing Company, *Irwin Professional* has been known and respected worldwide for innovation, quality and service in each of the key markets we serve. *Irwin Professional* is now positioned as the publisher of the largest and most diversified business and financial information product line in the book publishing industry. This position of strength and critical mass is vital in today's quickly evolving world of information delivery. We have the information you need and can provide it in the format you require.

To learn more about other *Irwin Professional* Banking publications, and to receive your copy of our complete publication and products catalog, please take a moment to complete this form and return it to the *Irwin Professional* Customer Service Department.

Four easy ways to return this information:
- **Call** our Customer Service Department toll-free: **1-800-634-3966**
- **Internet:** ipro @ irwin.com
- **Fax** toll-free: **1-800-926-9495**
- **Mail** to *Irwin Professional* Customer Service,
  **1333 Burr Ridge Parkway, Burr Ridge, IL 60521.**

Be sure to include code **1956** with your request for additional information.

---

## IRWIN
*Professional Publishing*®
**code 1956**

Name _____ Title _____

Organization _____ Address _____

Department/Floor/Suite _____

City _____ State _____ Zip _____

Telephone ( ) _____ FAX ( ) _____ E-mail _____

Did you purchase this book in a bookstore? Yes___No___If yes, please indicate the store/location. _____

What is the name and location of the bookstore where you primarily purchase professional reading materials?_____

Please indicate with a ✔ your areas of interest:
- ❏ Operations
- ❏ Compliance
- ❏ Fraud and Security
- ❏ Retail Banking
- ❏ Investment Management
- ❏ Executive Management
- ❏ Human Resources
- ❏ Treasury/Risk Management
- ❏ Trust Services
- ❏ Lending
- ❏ Finance and Accounting
- ❏ Other _____

Please send:
- ❏ the *Irwin Professional* Bank publication and products catalog
- ❏ my complementary issue of The *Irwin Professional* COMMUNITY BANKER
- ❏ information on upcoming seminars

bankfm 11.95

# INTEREST RATE VOLATILITY

## Understanding, Analyzing, and Managing Interest Rate Risk and Risk-Based Capital

*Gerald A. Hanweck*

*Bernard Shull*

**A BankLine Publication**

**IRWIN**

*Professional Publishing*®

Chicago • London • Singapore

HG
6024.5
H38
1996

## *A Bankline Publication*
## ◢ *IRWIN*
*Professional Publishing*®

© Richard D. Irwin, a Times Mirror Higher Education Group, Inc. company, 1996

*All rights reserved.* No part of this publication may be
reproduced, stored in a retrieval system, or transmitted,
in any form or by any means, electronic, mechanical,
photocopying, recording, or otherwise, without the prior
written permission of the publisher.

This publication is designed to provide accurate and
authoritative information in regard to the subject matter
covered. It is sold with the understanding that neither the
author nor the publisher is engaged in rendering legal, accounting,
or other professional service. If legal advice or other expert
assistance is required, the services of a competent professional
person should be sought.

*From a Declaration of Principles jointly adopted by a Committee*
*of the American Bar Association and a Committee of Publishers.*

◥▼ **Times Mirror**
**M  Higher Education Group**

**Library of Congress Cataloging–in–Publication Data**
Hanweck, Gerald A.
    Interest rate volatility  :   understanding, analyzing, and managing
interest rate risk and risk-based capital  /  Gerald A. Hanweck,
Bernard Shull.
        p.    cm.—(Bankline publication)
    Includes index.
    ISBN 1–55738–768–0
    1. Interest rate risk.   I. Shull, Bernard, 1931–    .  II. Title.
III. Series.
HG6024.5.H38   1996
332.63′23—dc20                                                          95–46010

*Printed in the United States of America*
1 2 3 4 5 6 7 8 9 0 BS 2 1 0 9 8 7 6 5

*To Barbara for her patience, Jerry Jr. for his insight,
and Julia and Gregory for their tolerance*

*Gerald A. Hanweck*


*To Janice, Abby, Ira and Joe*

*Bernard Shull*

# Contents

# Preface

Over the last 15 years, there has been serious concern among banks and bank regulators about fluctuations in interest rates and their effects on the value and viability of depository institutions. The concern grows out of the extraordinary interest rate volatility in the early 1980s that severely damaged the economy overall and financial institutions in particular. While commercial banks were not among the institutions that were irreparably harmed, savings and loans were. The threat to all depository institutions was apparent.

Much of the problem in the early 1980s has been attributed to inflationary expectations that developed during the 1970s, and a general loss of faith in the Federal Reserve's willingness to restrain inflationary increases in the money supply. Once the expectations were established, and the Fed decided that it must, at all costs, eradicate them and reestablish its credibility, it was compelled to permit interest rates to fluctuate widely.

Since the mid-1980s, the Federal Reserve has increasingly emphasized price level stability as a target of its operations. This has implied movements in interest rates to restrain or stimulate growth. Federal Reserve announcements of policy in the past several years have typically been in terms of whether short-term rates of interest are to rise, fall, or stay about the same. The Fed's expectations are that successfully restraining inflation will limit any rise in interest rates that would otherwise occur.

The idea that the Federal Reserve should manage interest rates to prevent inflation is an old one that had a large number of prestigious supporters among economists in the 1920s. It came into disfavor in the post–World War II period with the recognition that wide interest rate fluctuations would affect asset and capital values dramatically. The idea, however, is back, with the caveat of "depository institutions beware."

Depository institutions are obligated to protect themselves and their stockholders against interest rate movements that are planned by the Federal Reserve, and also those that are the result of unplanned and unexpected changes in economic activity and events. It is now widely understood that such fluctuations can have major effects on the value of their institutions. Congress knows this, and so do the federal bank regulatory agencies. Congress, in passing the Federal Deposit Insurance Corporation Improvement Act in 1991, made it clear that large deposit insurance fund losses imposed on tax-payers will no longer be tolerated. Capital requirements for insured banks must be, at least roughly, adjusted to the risks banks incur.

The federal banking agencies, under a directive from Congress, have been trying to incorporate interest rate risk into risk-based capital requirements for almost 5 years. They have had a notable lack of success. The problem is difficult and, as discussed here, the agencies have, for the time being, assumed a holding pattern; that is, they have informed banks that they have the authority to im-pose an additional capital charge on banks with "excessive" inter-est rate risk, and that they will let bank supervisors judge how much is needed on an *ad hoc* basis.

Though the regulators are, as yet, confounded as to how to de-termine precisely how much interest rate risk exposure is "exces-sive," and how much capital is necessary to protect the deposit in-surance funds from such risk, depository institutions cannot afford to be. They are the ones, regardless of any capital charges that the regulators might impose, who bear the brunt of fluctua-tions if they have not properly measured interest rate risk expo-sure and taken protective steps.

In this book we make an effort to illuminate the problem banks face in meeting both the demands of the market and the demands of the banking agencies. We do so by putting the problem—and the regulatory efforts intended to confront it—in historic perspec-tive. We consider the alternative ways of measuring interest rate risk and of modeling its impact on bank value. And we make a number of suggestions as to what enlightened bank management can do to protect itself against interest rate volatility and, at the same time, deal with the bank regulators. To this end, a supple-ment is available with spreadsheets for the calculation of interest rate risk exposure using the regulators' model. A diskette in Microsoft Excel 5.0 and Lotus 123 formats is included to facilitate computations. For more information, please call Irwin Professional Publishing Customer Service at 1-800-634-3966.

There was a time, in the not too distant past, when interest rate risk exposure was not a problem for banks. Experience in the early 1980s made clear that this was no longer the case. The memory of the volatile interest rate movements of those years may be waning, but the abrupt changes in rates in the early 1990s that wounded important financial and nonfinancial institutions indicate that interest rate risk difficulties are likely to persist indefinitely.

## Chapter One

# Introduction

The capacity of commercial banks and other depository institutions to issue short-term liabilities to individuals and businesses and then invest these funds in longer-term assets has been fundamental, over the past several hundred years, to their growth and success. The ability of banks to do so is made possible, in large part, by the fact that the variability of large numbers of independent deposit accounts is normally much lower than any one or small group of such accounts. Discovered by bankers centuries ago, this "law of large numbers" has permitted banks to carry mismatches without taking excessive risks.

Interest rate changes, however, particularly substantial increases, pose a unique threat to banking practice based on the principle. Because such changes affect everyone, depositors who would otherwise function independently are likely to respond collectively. In a competitive system, many will simultaneously require higher rates and/or withdraw their funds. Bank liquidity will be placed under pressure, and income is likely to fall. Interest rate increases also reduce the market value of fixed-rate assets, and similar effects can be expected on off–balance sheet positions based on the market value of such assets. On a market basis, then, banks' net worth will also fall. Thus, the mismatches that have always been an intrinsic element of bank success are also hazardous, as savings and loans (S&Ls), more than any other depository institutions, discovered in the 1980s.

From a bank's point of view, interest rate risk must be dealt with like other identifiable and interrelated risks to the value of net worth, including credit risk, concentration risk, liquidity risk, and country risk. From the point of view of the federal bank regulatory agencies, interest rate risk, like these others, poses a threat to bank solvency and, therefore, to the deposit insurance funds if the bank is not closed before the market value of its net worth becomes negative.

Congress has established special provisions in the law to cover the possible impact of interest rate changes on bank net worth and, in turn, the federal deposit insurance funds for which taxpayers have a contingent liability. The principal federal banking agencies—the Office of the Comptroller of the Currency (OCC), the Federal Reserve (Fed), the Federal Deposit Insurance Corporation (FDIC), and the Office of Thrift Supervision (OTS)—have been required under the FDIC Improvement Act of 1991 (FDICIA) to incorporate interest rate risk into existing capital requirements. Over the last several years there have been widespread discussions among bankers, bank regulators, and economists on what kinds of standards need to be established and how they should be implemented.

As in the case of all regulation, however, there are potential side effects, with the possibility of costs being greater than benefits, injuries imposed on those being regulated and, in the extreme, the regulation itself being ineffective or perverse. We undertake in the chapters that follow to review the recent efforts by the federal banking agencies to establish standards for regulating interest rate risk, to evaluate their likely effects, and to suggest alternatives that could benefit both banks and the public. In this first chapter, we introduce the subject with some preliminary definitions, a brief review of the recent problems that have led to the current efforts to regulate interest rate risk, and the legislative and regulatory framework within which these efforts are being undertaken.

## PRELIMINARY DEFINITION OF INTEREST RATE AND RELATED RISKS

Interest rate risk can be defined, as suggested above, as the risk that interest rate changes will reduce the market value of a bank through their direct effects on debt instruments, including financial assets, liabilities, and off–balance sheet positions.[1] These direct effects are closely associated with the maturities of assets and liabilities, and their cash flows over time. "Duration," an index number that takes maturities, cash flows, and their timing into consideration, has frequently been used to identify the effects of interest rate changes on the value of assets and liabilities and of banks.[2]

For the most part, we confine ourselves to the problems associated with the management and regulation of interest rate risk. It is necessary to acknowledge, however, that this risk is a subset of other risks. Interest rate changes also underlie many of the price changes of other financial instruments and activities with which banks are involved. "Market risk" is a more comprehensive concept than interest rate risk that includes the risk of losses to both on– and off–balance sheet positions arising from movements in all relevant market prices, including exchange rates, commodity prices, and equity prices, as well as interest rates.[3] Such price changes may be produced by movements in interest rates through economic channels not directly related to maturities or duration. Such movements may also impair the capacities of bank borrowers to repay their debts, and materialize as credit risk.

## RECENT BANKING PROBLEMS AND CHANGES IN LAW

The banking problems that flared up about 15 years ago are the background for current efforts to regulate interest rate risk. In perspective, they are the latest installment in a succession of periodic problems and reforms that have characterized banking in the United States. The evolution of the federal bank regulatory structure can be traced through a succession of crises. Each of the principal agencies—the OCC, the Fed, the FDIC, and the OTS—is a living artifact of responses to past episodes of serious banking distress. Each was intended, at least in part, to prevent reoccurrence by improving supervision and regulation. It is of some interest, as discussed in Chapter 2, that in none of these earlier episodes of crisis and reform has interest rate risk played a significant role.

The last 15 years, however, have been a different story. Interest rate risk did clearly play a role in the chronic difficulties encountered by S&Ls in the late 1970s and early 1980s. Even before the unprecedented increases in interest rates beginning in 1979 that were to raise prime rates to over 20 percent and mortgage rates to over 15 percent during the next several years, it had been clear that S&Ls were in a precarious position. In the 1960s and 1970s, market rates on short-term funds periodically rose above maximums on time and savings deposits permitted by Regulation Q. When this occurred, periods of "disintermediation" ensued, and the diminished market value of S&L net worth, resulting from the maturity mismatch on their balance sheets, was clearly revealed. But these periods were relatively short, and to a degree the impact on depository institutions could be controlled, at least temporarily, by the Federal Reserve's fine-tuning of Regulation Q that permitted S&Ls (and other depository institutions) to discriminate in favor of "hot money."

The high and volatile interest rates of 1979–82 that produced, at times, an inverted yield curve were, however, in the words of Edwin Gray, chairman of the Federal Home Loan Bank Board, a "holocaust." On a market value basis, they probably eliminated completely the net worth of almost all S&Ls. Figure 1–1 provides a picture of the volatility of interest rates during the period. Figure 1–2 indicates how unusual the rate levels were; they are unmatched on a monthly-average basis going back to the Civil War. The impact on the net worth of thrifts is shown in Table 1–1. The ratio of equity to assets had fallen below 3 percent on the basis of (non–market valued) "Generally Accepted Accounting Principles" (GAAP) in 1982.

The principal response of the Federal Home Loan Bank Board, the federal regulatory agency for S&Ls at the time, was not to close S&Ls that had become insolvent, but to "wait and see" if interest rates would not soon fall, and to broaden permissible investment activities to permit them to "go for broke"; that is, to "gamble for resurrection." As is well known, the strategy proved a disaster. In Table 1–2, the decline of the thrift industry in the 1980s is depicted in declining income and rising numbers of failures. But this, of course, was just the beginning. Resolution of insolvent thrifts after 1989 left the industry decimated. In 1980, there had been about 4,000 insured S&Ls. Currently, there are fewer than half that number and the future holds little promise for those that remain.

Commercial bank failures also rose to unusually high levels in the 1980s. In 1980, only 10 insured banks, with about $216 million

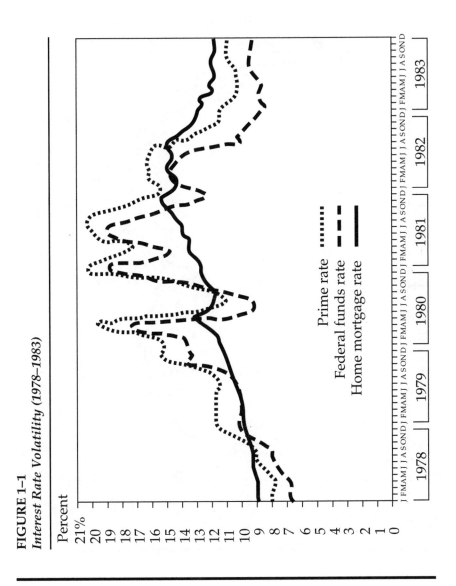

**FIGURE 1-1**
*Interest Rate Volatility (1978–1983)*

in deposits, failed. In 1985, the number had reached 120, with $8 billion in deposits; and in 1989, it had reached 206, with $24 billion in deposits. Over the decade as a whole, over 1,000 insured banks, with about $92 billion in deposits, failed. While it does not appear that interest rate risk played an important role in these failures,

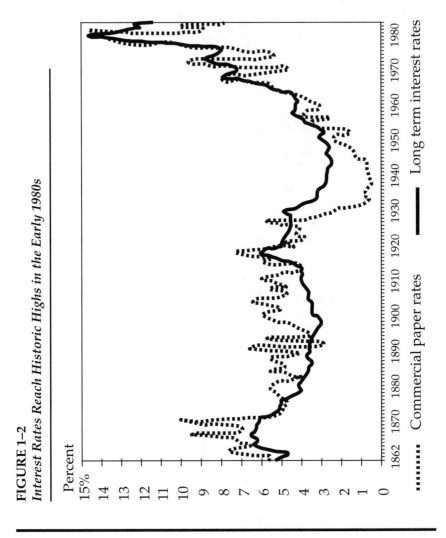

**FIGURE 1-2**
*Interest Rates Reach Historic Highs in the Early 1980s*

Percent

15%
14
13
12
11
10
9
8
7
6
5
4
3
2
1
0

1862 1870 1880 1890 1900 1910 1920 1930 1940 1950 1960 1970 1980

•••••••• Commercial paper rates

⸻ Long term interest rates

the federal regulatory agencies became concerned about the levels of capital they held. They imposed "leverage requirements" (minimum ratios of capital to assets) in the early 1980s. By the end of the decade, they had established risk-based capital requirements in conjunction with an international agreement that had been worked out with other major industrialized countries (the Basle Accord of 1988).[4]

**TABLE 1–1**
*Thrift Net Worth[a]*

| | Net Worth ($ Billions) | | | Net Worth to Assets Ratio (%) | | |
|---|---|---|---|---|---|---|
| Year | RAP[b] | GAAP[c] | Tangible[d] | RAP[b] | GAAP[c] | Tangible[d] |
| 1980 | $32 | $32 | $32 | 5.30% | 5.30% | 5.30% |
| 1981 | 28 | 27 | 25 | 4.38 | 4.22 | 3.91 |
| 1982 | 26 | 20 | 4 | 3.79 | 2.92 | 0.58 |
| 1983 | 33 | 25 | 4 | 4.05 | 3.07 | 0.49 |
| 1984 | 37 | 27 | 3 | 3.78 | 2.76 | 0.31 |
| 1985 | 47 | 34 | 9 | 4.39 | 3.18 | 0.84 |
| 1986 | 53 | 39 | 15 | 4.55 | 3.35 | 1.29 |
| 1987 | 51 | 34 | 9 | 4.08 | 2.72 | 0.72 |
| 1988 | 61 | 46 | 23 | 4.51 | 3.40 | 1.70 |

[a]Thrifts are defined as FSLIC-insured institutions and associations and other savings banks.
[b]RAP net worth is based on regulatory accounting principles.
[c]GAAP net worth is based on Generally Accepted Accounting Principles.
[d]Tangible net worth is equal to GAAP net worth minus intangible assets, principally goodwill.
Source: James R. Barth, Philip F. Bartholomew and Carol J. Labich, "Moral Hazard and the Thrift Crisis: An Analysis of 1988 Resolutions," *Research Paper #160*, Office of Policy and Economic Research, Federal Home Loan Bank Board, May 1989, pp. 2–9.

Regulatory reform and reorganization in the United States was initiated by the Financial Institutions Reform, Recovery and Enforcement Act of 1989 (FIRREA) and expanded by FDICIA in 1991. FIRREA in 1989 was necessitated by the need to close and resolve large numbers of insolvent S&Ls and reorganize their deposit insurance fund. FDICIA was a response to rising rates of commercial bank failures, and near depletion of the FDIC's bank insurance fund. FIRREA and FDICIA are the most recent efforts in the long line of reforms aimed at making sure that "it never happens again."[5]

A principal element of both laws has, as noted, been the establishment of risk-based capital requirements. These classify bank assets within broad risk-weight categories and thereby differentiate them on the basis of their default risk. Risk weights are then used as multipliers to calculate the total volume of risk-adjusted

**TABLE 1–2**
*Thrift Industry in the 1980s*

| Year | Number of Institutions* | Total Assets ($Billions) | Net Income ($Millions) | Number of Failures | Number of Insolvent Institutions |
|------|------|------|------|------|------|
| 1980 | 3,993 | $  604 | $   781 | 32 | 43 |
| 1981 | 3,751 | 640 | (4,631) | 82 | 87 |
| 1982 | 3,287 | 686 | (4,142) | 247 | 237 |
| 1983 | 3,146 | 814 | 1,945 | 70 | 293 |
| 1984 | 3,136 | 978 | 1,022 | 36 | 445 |
| 1985 | 3,246 | 1,070 | 3,728 | 63 | 470 |
| 1986 | 3,220 | 1,164 | 131 | 80 | 471 |
| 1987 | 3,147 | 1,251 | (7,779) | 77 | 520 |
| 1988 | 2,949 | 1,352 | (12,057) | 247 | 364 |

Thrifts are defined as FSLIC-insured institutions and include savings and loan associations and other savings banks. The number of failures includes liquidations, assisted mergers, supervisory mergers, management consignment cases, and stabilization. The number of insolvent FSLIC-insured institutions is based on Generally Accepted Accounting Principles (GAAP).

*Year-end figures.

Source: James R. Barth, Philip F. Bartholomew and Carol J. Labich, "Moral Hazard and the Thrift Crisis: An Analysis of 1988 Resolutions," Office of Policy and Economic Research, Federal Home Loan Bank Board, May 1989, pp. 2–9.

assets held by the bank. Capital requirements are then specified as a percentage of risk-weighted assets.[6] Risk-based capital requirements, already developed for commercial banks, were required for S&Ls by FIRREA. These requirements are intended to prevent banks from taking advantage of the implicit subsidization of risk in the existing "safety net" provisions (in particular, deposit insurance and "lender of last resort" assistance from the Fed) under current law. Further, they initiate a uniform basis for capital regulation among competitive institutions.

The risk-based capital standards were initially developed only for credit risk; that is, the risk that a particular class of loan or investment, such as a residential mortgage loan or a government security or a commercial loan, would default. But FDICIA also requires that other risks be incorporated into capital requirements, including interest rate risk. The federal bank regulatory agencies have made proposals to comply.[7] An interest rate risk proposal has been issued, and a final rule promulgated.

In any discussion of the threat posed to depository institutions by interest rate changes, it is well to keep in mind the theme with which this chapter began: that when interest rates changes align themselves in the "right" way, they can bestow great benefits on depository institutions. Changes in conditions over the past several years are testimony to this fact. The condition of depository institutions and, in particular, commercial banks has improved remarkably. Much of the improvement has been traceable to the development of an unusually wide spread between long- and short-term interest rates that has permitted banks to earn substantial profits. The dramatic increase in the spread between 1989 and 1992 is shown in Figure 1–3. Bank profits have increased accordingly, and the number of banks failing has declined substantially. In 1994, only 11 banks failed, the lowest number since 1981.[8] On March 31, 1995, over 98 percent of all insured commercial banks were classified as well capitalized, and only about 0.1 percent were classified as critically undercapitalized (Table 1–3).

## PROPOSALS FOR REGULATING INTEREST RATE RISK

In September 1993, the federal banking agencies issued a Notice of Proposed Rulemaking (NPR) to integrate interest rate risk into risk-based capital requirements.[9] The proposal outlined an approach aimed at reducing the exposure of the federal deposit insurance fund—and, beyond the fund—taxpayers, emanating from interest rate volatility and its effects on the economic value of bank equity. It would have required banks identified as having relatively high levels of interest rate risk to increase their equity capital.

In August 1995, the agencies issued a "Final Rule." The "Rule" was accompanied by a "Joint Policy Statement" on measuring interest rate risk.[10] The Rule and Statement, unlike the 1993 NPR, do not establish a formal basis for levying a capital charge. They are discussed in detail in Chapter 6. In the Appendix to this book, a computer-based spreadsheet for computing interest rate risk, using the agencies' model and format is provided.

**FIGURE 1–3**
*Treasury Yield Spread, (10-Year T-Bond) – (2-Year T-Bond) (Daily, January 2, 1984, to June 30, 1994)*

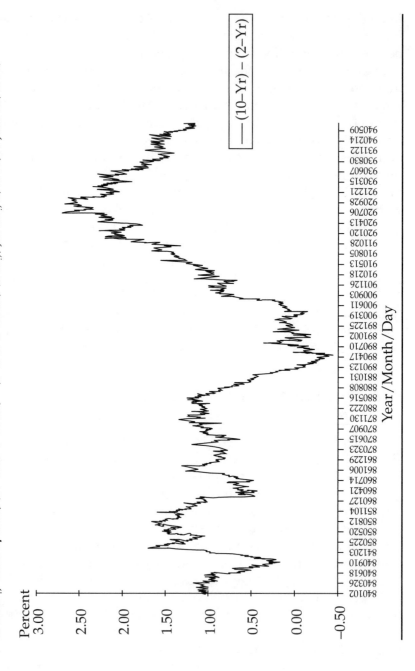

**TABLE 1-3**
*Capital Category Distribution\* (Insured Commercial Banks)*

|  | Number | Percent of Total | Assets ($Billions) | Percent of Total |
|---|---|---|---|---|
| *September 30, 1992* | | | | |
| Well capitalized | 10,942 | 94.4% | $2,685 | 77.1% |
| Adequately capitalized | 455 | 3.9 | 746 | 21.4 |
| Undercapitalized | 109 | 1.0 | 34 | 1.0 |
| Significantly undercapitalized | 47 | 0.4 | 8 | 0.2 |
| Critically undercapitalized | 87 | 0.3 | 8 | 0.2 |
| *March 31, 1995* | | | | |
| Well capitalized | 10,408 | 98.2% | $4,250.9 | 97.3% |
| Adequately capitalized | 120 | 1.4 | 115.6 | 2.6 |
| Undercapitalized | 12 | 0.2 | 1.1 | 0.0 |
| Significantly undercapitalized | 6 | 0.1 | 0.8 | 0.0 |
| Critically undercapitalized | 8 | 0.1 | 0.4 | 0.0 |

\*For definitions of capital categories, see Table 1-4.

Source: FDIC, Division of Research and Statistics. Tables are based solely on call report data and do not reflect supervisory upgrades or downgrades.

In April of 1995, the Basle Committee on Bank Supervision proposed to supplement its 1988 Capital Accord to cover market risk.[11] The 1988 accord provides the conceptual basis for current risk-based capital requirements in the United States. The new proposal is applicable to large, internationally active banks and carves out the risks pertaining to on– and off–balance sheet positions arising from price movements for debt securities and equities in their trading books, and also to foreign exchange and commodities risk throughout their operations. It does not address the problem of interest rate risk throughout, a question to which the Committee promises to return, and it applies to only a relatively few large banks in the United States.

The new Basle proposal does provide a conceptual approach for defining and integrating interest rate risk that is likely to be influential.[12] The approach is, moreover, consistent with the proposal put forward by the federal banking agencies in 1993. It is possible that the federal agency and Basle approaches will converge as the basis for future interest rate risk regulation of banks in the United States.

The proper integration of interest rate risk into risk-based capital requirements is particularly important within the framework of FDICIA because risk-based requirements are a key element in its provisions for "prompt corrective action."[13] Any interest rate risk provision can have the effect of moving banks from a higher to a lower level of capital acceptance and bringing about regulatory intervention of one type or another.

Under the current "prompt corrective action" arrangements, five classes of capital adequacy were specified as thresholds to activate supervisory intervention (Table 1–4). Four have been defined by the federal agencies. These include "significantly undercapitalized," "undercapitalized," "adequately capitalized," and "well capitalized."[14] The law specifies a terminal requirement of tangible equity to total assets of 2 percent for critically undercapitalized institutions.

A regulatory determination that a bank is not well or adequately capitalized triggers restrictions that escalate as the bank falls into the lower capital classifications. Of particular importance for a bank in one of the lower classifications is the requirement that it submit an acceptable capital restoration plan (Title I, Section 131). A bank falling into the critically undercapitalized classification must be closed promptly. (A more complete description of the escalating restrictions can be found in Table 1–5.)

## PURPOSE AND SCOPE OF BOOK

The capital requirements established for interest rate risk are critical to commercial banks and other depository institutions. If excessive, they will impede their efficient operations. If deficient, they will jeopardize the deposit insurance fund. If based on faulty considerations, they may do both.

In this book we evaluate the regulatory agency efforts of recent years to meet the requirements that have been established by recent legislation, and draw inferences as to the likely effects on

**TABLE 1–4**
*Capital Levels Established for Prompt Corrective Action*

| Capital Classification | Characteristics |
| --- | --- |
| Well capitalized | Total risk-based capital at least 10%<br>Tier 1 risk-based capital ratio of at least 6%<br>Leverage ratio of at least 5% |
| Adequately capitalized | Total risk-based capital at least 8%<br>Tier 1 risk-based capital ratio at least 4%<br>Leverage ratio of at least 4% (3% for top-rated institutions not experiencing or anticipating significant growth) |
| Undercapitalized | Fails to meet one or more of the required minimum capital levels needed to be classified as adequately capitalized, but not significantly or critically undercapitalized. |
| Significantly undercapitalized | Total risk-based capital less than 6%; or<br>Tier 1 risk-based capital ratio less than 3%; or<br>Leverage ratio of less than 3% |
| Critically undercapitalized | Tangible equity-to-total assets ratio of 2% or less* |

*Tangible equity is a newly defined term which combines elements of core capital and cumulative perpetual preferred stock minus all intangible assets except for limited amounts of purchased mortgage servicing rights.

Source: Adapted from FDIC, Office of Inspector General, "Audit of FDIC's Implementation of the Prompt Corrective Action Provisions of FDICIA," September 23, 1994.

bank profits and growth. In subsequent chapters, we highlight the problems created by attempting to integrate interest rate risk into risk-based capital requirements, and propose alternative methods intended to satisfy the needs of both the regulators and the banks.

In Chapter 2, the problem of interest rate risk is discussed in historic perspective, and in Chapter 3, we review public policy responses to the relatively recent recognition of interest rate risk. In Chapter 4, we describe and evaluate the principal methods for measuring interest rate risk, and consider alternative approaches. In Chapter 5, we describe and evaluate the models used to judge the impact of interest rate risk, and propose alternative methods. In Chapter 6, we review the practical problems encountered by the

**TABLE 1–5**
*Restrictions on Banks in Lower Capital Classifications*

Restrictions on Undercapitalized Banks

Must file a capital restoration plan within 45 days of the date it receives notice that it is undercapitalized.

Subject to automatic restrictions on capital distribution and management fees, asset growth restrictions, and prohibitions against making acquisitions, opening branches, or engaging in new lines of business without the prior approval of its primary regulator.

Other, harsher restrictions may be imposed on a case-by-case basis.

Restrictions on Significantly Undercapitalized Banks

Subject to restrictions that automatically apply to undercapitalized institutions, plus other limitations, including mandatory prohibitions against the payment of bonuses and raises to senior officers without the regulator's prior approval.

Restrictions on Critically Undercapitalized Banks

Subject to restrictions that apply to undercapitalized and significantly undercapitalized institutions plus other prohibitions which may be imposed by the FDIC.

Prohibited from the following without FDIC approval: Entering into material transactions other than usual course of business;

Extending credit for any highly leveraged transaction;

Amending its charter or bylaws except to the extent necessary to carry out any requirement by law;

Making any material change in its accounting methods;

Engaging in any covered transaction covered by section 23A(b) of the Federal Reserve Act;

Paying excessive bonuses or compensation;

Paying interest on new or renewed liabilities at a rate which would increase the institution's weighted average cost of funds to a level significantly exceeding the prevailing rates in the institution's normal market areas; and

Paying principal or interest on the institution's subordinated debt beginning 60 days after becoming critically undercapitalized.

Institutions that fall below the 2% tangible equity level must be placed in conservatorship or receivership within 90 days of becoming critically undercapitalized, unless an extension is granted. Agency discretionary restrictions are imposed by means of a "prompt corrective action" directive.

Source: Adapted from FDIC, Office of Inspector General, "Audit of FDIC's Implementation of the Prompt Corrective Action Provisions of FDICIA," September 23, 1994.

federal banking agencies in trying to integrate interest rate risk into risk-based capital requirements. In Chapter 7, we summarize our findings and consider prospects for the agencies and the banks. A supplement is available that provides spreadsheets on diskette to facilitate the computation of a bank's interest rate risk according to the federal regulators' model. For more information, please call Irwin Professional Publishing Customer Service at 1-800-634-3966.

The attempt to incorporate interest rate risk into risk-based capital requirements reflects a diagnosis of the problems recently experienced. The effectiveness of reform will depend on whether the diagnosis is sound. We suggest in what follows that with respect to interest rate risk, reform has given too much weight to the problems of S&Ls that were, in large part, a product of a rigid legal structure that had required significant mismatches, impacted by changing market conditions. The S&L interest rate risk problems were exacerbated by a regulatory establishment that did not fully appreciate the effects of its policies. In attempting to preserve an industry whose equity had eroded, through policies of forbearance, and to promote accelerated growth, the Federal Home Loan Bank Board ignored the moral hazard of trusting managers without anything to lose, and the resulting credit quality problems. The subsequent "debacle" may well have contributed to an exaggerated concern about the impact of changing interest rates on the viability of depository institutions.

If the diagnosis is not sound, the remedy—in this case, higher capital requirements—is likely to be flawed also. It is of some interest that 25 years ago, capital requirements were considered by a number of sophisticated observers to be a dubious instrument for regulating banks and controlling the risks they incur.[15] Today, capital requirements are seen as the single most important instrument in the regulatory arsenal. The approach taken by the Basle Committee and the federal banking agencies today is that all risks can be translated into something comparable to "credit risk," and subjected to an appropriate capital charge that will provide bank supervisors, in a risky world where interest rates can suddenly rise and stock markets can crash, with "sufficient comfort."[16]

The methodology for translating interest rate risk into an appropriate capital charge, however, has proved elusive. The failure of the federal banking agencies to promptly meet the legal requirements of FDICIA suggests the existence of serious difficulties. The existence of such difficulties is often a warning that the concepts need to be rethought. There are reasons to believe that the approach now being elaborated stretches capital requirements beyond the point where they can function beneficially. A rethinking of the issue is undertaken here.

## NOTES

1. See Benton Gup and Robert Brooke, *Interest Rate Risk Management,* Probus/Richard D. Irwin, Chicago/Burr Ridge, IL, 1993, p. 5.
2. Duration and other concepts to measure the exposure of banks to interest rate risk are discussed in detail in Chapter 4.
3. Basle Committee on Banking Supervision, "The Prudential Supervision of Netting, Market Risks and Interest Rate Risk," April 1993.
4. Risk-based capital requirements were established for U.S. banks and bank holding companies in January 1989 on the basis of the framework established by the Basle Committee in July of 1988. (The Basle Committee on Banking Supervision is a committee of banking supervisory authorities which was established by central banks of the Group of Ten countries that meets at the Bank for International Settlements in Basle.) The "Final Risk-Based Capital Guidelines" established by the Federal banking agencies in the U.S. were published under a Federal Reserve press release of January 19, 1989. They became effective in final form on December 31, 1992.
5. FDICIA emerged out of a comprehensive Treasury proposal that also included relaxation of restrictions on interstate branching, permitting banks to engage more fully in securities and insurance activities, and allowing bank holding companies to be owned by commercial firms (U.S. Treasury Department, 1991). The deregulation provisions of the proposal were deferred by Congress in passing FDICIA. In 1994, however, the Riegle-Neal Interstate Banking and Branching Efficiency Act, permitting nationwide branching, was passed. A review of the problems that resulted in the passage of FIRREA and FDICIA can be found in the recent report of the National Commission on Financial Institutions Reform, Recovery and Enforcement, *Origins and Causes of the S&L Debacle: A Blueprint for Reform,* A Report to the President and Congress of the U.S., June, 1993.
6. Off–balance sheet items are converted to a dollar value equivalent, multiplied by the appropriate risk weight and added to risk-adjusted assets.

7. Other risks for which capital is required by Section 305 of FDICIA are concentration risk and nontraditional activity risk. A notice revising risk-based standards to incorporate these risks was issued in February 1994: Federal Reserve, "Press Release on Risk-Based Capital Standards: Concentration of Credit Risk and Risks of Nontraditional Activities," February 17, 1994.

8. The Bank Insurance Fund (BIF) was established by FIRREA as the successor to the former FDIC insurance fund principally for commercial banks.

9. Federal Reserve, "Press Release on Revising Risk-Based Capital Standards: Interest Rate Risk," September 15, 1993.

10. "Risk-Based Capital Standards: Interest Rate Risk," Federal Register, Rules and Regulations, Vol. 60, No. 148, August 2, 1995, pp. 39490–39571.

11. Basle Committee on Banking Supervision, "Planned Supplement to the Capital Accord to Incorporate Market Risks," April 1995, p. 1.

12. The Fed, the OCC, and the FDIC have submitted a Notice of Proposed Rulemaking seeking formal comment on the Basle proposal.

13. "Prompt corrective action," requiring intervention by the appropriate federal banking agency in accordance with a bank's capital ratios, is also required by FDICIA. The current rules for "prompt corrective action" are described in detail in Federal Reserve Board, "Press Release on 'Prompt Corrective Action,' " September 18, 1992.

14. The final rules of the federal banking agencies on the definitions of the capital classifications went into effect on December 19, 1992. See Federal Reserve Press Release, September 18, 1992.

15. For an earlier view toward capital requirements that is fascinating in its divergence from current views, see the monograph by George Vojta, then Vice President for Corporate Planning at Citibank (formerly First National City Bank), *Bank Capital Adequacy*, First National City Bank, February 1973.

16. In its recent report, the Basle Committee notes that "[m]any of the factors . . . are very difficult to quantify. Even if they were capable of quantification, a judgement would still have to be made as to how far it is necessary to guard against rare market occurrences. The conclusion of the Committee is that supervisors would not have sufficient comfort unless the value-at-risk measure . . . set out in this section, were to be multiplied by an appropriate factor. . . . The *multiplication factor* will be set by individual supervisors . . . subject to an absolute minimum of 3." See Basle Committee on Banking Supervision, "An Internal Model-Based Approach to Market Risk Capital Requirements," April 1995, p. 15.

*Chapter Two*

# Interest Rate Fluctuations and Public Policy in Perspective

Interest rate issues, other than the interest rate risk, have been a focal point of public policy for many years. Bankers, government officials, and economists have, from time to time, viewed rising, falling, fluctuating, and even stable interest rates as serious problems to be addressed by public policy. It may seem surprising, then, that only in recent years have the effects of interest rate changes on bank viability been considered a problem for bank regulation.[1]

The absence of earlier concerns can be traced to the different institutional conditions within which banking business was conducted in earlier years. Interest rate risk, it is suggested below, is a public policy problem of the late 20th century. In considering how the federal regulatory agencies may best deal with it now, it is useful to understand why it wasn't very important in the past, and how the current problem has emerged in the recent economic environment.

## EARLIER INTEREST RATE CONCERNS

Rising interest rates have periodically threatened the ability of governments, businesses, and farmers to obtain the credit they needed at acceptable costs, and have repeatedly been the subject of political agitation and legislative action. In the latter part of the 19th century, falling interest rates on government securities made the issuance of national bank notes relatively unprofitable and cut note circulation in half between 1880 and 1890.[2] At the same time, seasonal swings in interest rates, resulting from alterations in credit demands in farm areas and around Christmas time, were generally considered economically and financially disruptive by businesses and farmers.[3] Frequent crises in the latter part of the 19th century were also characterized by substantial fluctuations in interest rates. During such periods, banks were compelled to suspend the conversion of deposits into currency, and bank credit became difficult or impossible to obtain. An extreme example of credit stringency for stock market loans occurred in the fall of 1873 when call money rates rose to 61 percent; commercial paper rates rose to over 16 percent. During the crisis of 1907, call money rates exceeded 20 percent, and commercial paper rates increased from 5.44 percent in June to 7.83 in December.[4] The problems were seen as resulting from an "inelasticity of currency." From the point of view of banks, the problem was one of liquidity, that is, obtaining the funds (currency) needed to meet depositors' legal demands.

The Federal Reserve Act was passed in 1913 to solve such problems. By providing a new and "elastic" currency and by discounting commercial loans at its discount window, it was believed that the Federal Reserve could moderate seasonal interest rate volatility and forestall crises. The Fed was successful in smoothing out seasonal swings in interest rates in the 1920s, but it was not successful in preventing the banking crises of the next decade.[5]

In the 1920s, many economists argued that there was a danger that interest rates would be insufficiently flexible upward. Sluggishly rising rates during periods of expansion, they believed, were an underlying cause of inflation and subsequent recessions. They proposed that the Federal Reserve should aim to stabilize the price level by managing increases in interest rates during cyclical expansions.[6]

The reasoning of this group was succinctly summarized by John R. Commons, the University of Wisconsin economist who was one of the first to construct a price index: "[I]f we are to have stability of the general credit situation, which means relative stability of the general price level, then we cannot have stability of the rate of interest on money." If the Treasury (or other borrowers) had to pay more, so be it.[7] No adverse effect on banks was contemplated.

The Federal Reserve did appear to manage short-term interest rates to meet a price stability objective through much of the 1920's, and prices were in fact stable.[8]

## DEPRESSION CONCERNS AND THEREAFTER

Concerns about the way in which interest rates had been managed in the 1920s began to emerge in the 1930s. John Maynard Keynes, the most influential economist of the time, argued that economic expansions rarely achieved full employment and that it would be a mistake to choke off a boom by raising the rate of interest. He observed that rates in the United States should have fallen, rather than risen, in 1928 and 1929, to encourage new investment. "Thus an increase in the rate of interest, as a remedy for the state of affairs arising out of a prolonged period of abnormally heavy new investment, belongs to the species of remedy which cures the disease by killing the patient."[9]

The Keynesian analysis had other implications that, at the time, were not seen as particularly applicable to commercial banks but have subsequently become so. An integral idea was that consumers and businesses would, at some times, hold substantial amounts of cash, which paid no interest; that is, that they had a "liquidity preference." Underlying this "preference" for cash were the expectations of market participants about future asset values and the confidence with which they held such expectations. Interest rates might rise and bond values fall; in an uncertain world, holding cash provided rewards independent of interest payments.

The Keynesian distrust of interest rate fluctuations to achieve economic stability was elaborated in the 1950s by the Harvard economist Alvin Hansen, a principal interpreter of Keynes in the United States. He and others suggested that "[a]nalogous to the thinking which found price stability in wage instability is the theory that stability of the commodity price level can be achieved by a deliberate fluctuation, even a violent fluctuation, in security prices and capital values".[10] "One form of instability is used to fight another, and the instability deliberately introduced is allegedly unobjectionable—despite the vast changes in society's economic fabric—since it presumably helps to produce a 'higher' stability."[11] The "changes in society's economic fabric" included the extensive development of capital instruments and markets. To Hansen, this meant that "[n]owadays it is not possible . . . to stabilize commodity prices via interest-rate policy without causing instability in capital values. . . . No central banker is prepared to bring down upon the economy a collapse of capital values."

The sectors Hansen saw as endangered by higher interest rates (and "a collapse of capital values") included "stable industries," presumably like automobile manufacturing, farming, and services; small and growing businesses without large internal sources of funds; and state and local governments.[12] He did not include financial institutions among the endangered species.

## INTEREST RATES AND THE REVIVAL OF MONETARY POLICY

Robert Roosa, a vice president at the Federal Reserve Bank of New York, was a principal strategist of the new monetary policy that emerged in the post–World War II period. His views reflect what, for the time, was a unique combination of sophisticated economic analysis and financial market pragmatism. He recognized that banks had extended the maturities of their assets considerably since the pre-Depression years. In 1948, less than 50 percent of the earning assets held by commercial banks had maturities of less than 1 year.[13] The longer-term securities included government debt, mortgages, and term loans.

Roosa recognized that central bank interest rate policy had been viewed by many as "the touchstone of economic stability."[14] He agreed that interest rate policy involving large swings in rates was less acceptable than it once had been, principally because it was not likely to be effective. Contemporary research indicated that neither borrowers nor savers were as sensitive to interest rate changes as economists had once thought. He suggested that secular growth in internal financing had insulated businesses from the effects of such changes:

> At one time it was thought that changes in market rates of interest provided a satisfactory explanation—and central bank control over

rates an adequate corrective—for cyclical economic disturbance. . . . Economists . . . long believed that the significance of market rates of interest . . . lay in the effects produced upon borrowers, and upon *savers*. Little if any attention was given to lenders. . . . As experience and direct investigation revealed a rather wide range of indifference to rate changes among borrowers, and suggested that saving was closely related to such other factors as changes in income, there was an understandable slackening in the enthusiasm for central bank control over rates as a positive method of moderating cyclical fluctuation.

He further admitted that the Federal Reserve was limited in varying rates widely, and particularly in raising rates, because of the likely disruptive effects on the economy in general and the Treasury in particular.

Presumably, a limitation on the range of interest rate fluctuations is implied by the existence of a large public debt because the rate variations typical in the twenties and earlier would, in the new circumstances, set off a cumulative unloading or acquisition of debt instruments that would have harmful repercussions throughout the economy and might perhaps (in the event of unloading) impair the Government's credit. It is this fundamental concern, rather than the Treasury's outlays for debt service, that makes a return to widely fluctuating rates unlikely. . . . (Robert Roosa, "Interest Rates and the Central Bank," in *Money, Trade and Economic Growth: Essays in Honor of J. H. Williams*, Macmillan, New York, 1951)

Looking back from the present, it would seem a small step for Roosa to have then considered the potentially damaging effects of rising interest rates on the condition of commercial banks. In 1951, however, it was not a small step, and he did not. Rather, he saw the new bank holdings of longer-term assets as a change that would boost the effectiveness of monetary policy without seriously injuring banks, while simultaneously constraining interest rate volatility.

He concluded that the Federal Reserve's interest rate management would still work. A policy of restraint would increase short-term rates and reduce the willingness of lenders to make short-term credit available. It would also affect expectations about long-term rates and thereby increase these rates and the availability of long-term credit. Relatively small reductions in the value of longer-term assets held by banks would, then, have a "lock-in" effect, and keep interest rates from having to change very much to have the desired effect on the availability of credit. The focus of monetary policy, he believed, had shifted from fluctuations in interest rates to fluctuations in the availability of credit.[15]

The key to the analysis was his view that even a fraction of a percent increase would have considerable restraining effects on lending policies of banks. At the market rates then existing, even an eighth or a quarter of 1% increase in long-term rates would result in a substantial percentage decrease in market value of long-term securities. But even without a substantial decrease in value, he believed that there was "a widespread phobia [among bankers] concerning capital losses on security sales. . . . [E]ven among large lending institutions, a mathematical demonstration of the long-run gain from such switches is rejected because the impact of the capital loss on current income is considered too great. Thus a slight rise in yields on Governments may 'freeze in' many current holders. . . ."[16] In light of the experience of financial institutions in the last decade, it is illuminating to ask how Roosa could find that banks might entertain a "phobia" on realized capital losses that would outweigh profit opportunities, and that this behavior would not have a significant impact on bank solvency. The circumstances of the time that made this view plausible are discussed below.

## EMERGENCE OF INTEREST RATE RISK: DISINTERMEDIATION

The problems of interest rate risk began to emerge, as noted in Chapter 1, about a decade after Roosa published his analysis, particularly through the impact of rising rates on S&Ls. The problem developed as banks and S&Ls became exposed to intense deposit competition, including institutional innovations, like money market funds, aimed at circumventing the anticompetitive restrictions on deposit rates of interest established by law and regulation. From the mid-1960s and through the 1970s, Congress and the regulatory agencies tried to paper over these difficulties by new policies to prop up the old arrangements.[17]

By the mid-1960s, the interest rate risk embedded in S&L balance sheets was apparent. The first crisis occurred in 1965. With market rates above the maximums permitted on CDs, the Federal Reserve understood that an increase in Regulation Q maximums was needed to permit commercial banks to roll over maturing deposits. But it feared that the higher rates would result in substantial outflows of funds from S&Ls and savings banks that could, at the time, not "afford" to pay them, and could not easily raise funds by selling their lower-rate mortgages, for which no organized secondary market existed. Congress and the banking agencies attacked the problem as one of excessive competition among different types of depository institutions. Regulation Q maximums were imposed on S&Ls for the first time by the Interest Rate Adjustment Act of 1966. The regulatory suppression of price competition among depository institutions, however, did not resolve the interest rate risk problem embedded in S&L portfolios; depository institutions as a group faced competition from market instruments like Treasury bills and from other unregulated financial institutions. The most dramatic intensification of competition, aimed directly at circumventing Regulation Q, was the invention of the money market mutual fund in the early 1970s.

The effort of the government to suppress competition for deposits thus channeled the interest rate risk confronting individual institutions into an industrywide problem termed "disintermediation." When Regulation Q maximums were not increased rapidly enough to meet market competition, all depository institutions would lose funds to the market (and newly developed money market mutual funds). Fine-tuning of Regulation Q was intended to alleviate disintermediation and support depository institutions. The effect on the condition of banks and S&Ls became a problem to be dealt with by further regulation rather than by risk management.

As is now well known, regulatory refinements proved incapable of warding off the pressures of inflation and rising rates of interest in the late 1970s. The only solution seemed the elimination of Regulation Q. This was accomplished in the Depository Institutions Deregulation and Monetary Control Act of 1980

(DIDMCA), which provided for a phaseout over a six-year period—but not before the unprecedented rise in interest rates beginning in the late 1970s pushed most S&Ls into insolvency.

The unusual interest rate behavior in the 1979–82 period partly reflects accelerating inflation in the 1970s and rising inflationary expectations. But it is also partly attributable to changes in Federal Reserve policy. In the fall of 1979, the Fed altered its past practices (at least during the post–World War II period), of constraining interest rate movements, for the sake of better control over money supply growth. Not only did the amplitude of interest rate movements increase, as noted above, but interest rate changes became unpredictable.

The difficulty of predicting interest rate changes in the early 1980s is indicated by economic forecasts of the time that invariably proved seriously wrong. In Table 2–1, a well-known economic forecast (UCLA National Business Forecast) is compared with actual interest rates. As can be seen, the underestimation of actual rates through 1981 is dramatic. The percentage difference between actual and forecasted rates was consistently in double digits; and in a number of quarters, the difference was greater than 50 percent.

In earlier years, high interest rates had meant disintermediation. Construction and housing suffered because mortgage funds dried up. Even prior to 1980, however, Regulation Q restrictions had been substantially relaxed. In 1978 and 1979, S&Ls were in a position to pay market rates for funds that they otherwise might lose to the market. The result was that their costs skyrocketed relative to their earnings. Mortgage rates simultaneously increased, and both thrifts and the construction industry suffered severe losses. Many projects newly completed or under construction could not be sold. With developers walking away from properties, S&Ls and some banks were left with substantial amounts of "real estate owned" on their balance sheets. As noted in Chapter 1, failures of S&Ls rose, their income declined, and the value of their net worth eroded.

The initial problems were compounded by S&Ls and their regulators who failed to come to grips quickly with the new conditions. In the late 1970s, with rising interest rates, recognition of the newly emerging interest rate risk problem suggested a need for S&Ls to diversify their resources, and particularly to invest in

**TABLE 2-1**
*Interest Rate Forecasts (1979–1982)*

| Forecast Date | Forecast Period | Prime Rate | | | Aaa Corporate Bond Rate | | |
|---|---|---|---|---|---|---|---|
| | | *Forecast* | *Actual* | *Percent Difference* | *Forecast* | *Actual* | *Percent Difference* |
| December 1978 | 1st Q 1979 | 11.60% | 11.75% | -1.28% | 9.50% | 9.29% | 2.22% |
| | 2nd Q 1979 | 10.50 | 11.72 | -10.38 | 9.30 | 9.39 | -0.96 |
| | 3rd Q 1979 | 8.70 | 12.12 | -28.20 | 8.80 | 9.29 | -5.27 |
| | 4th Q 1979 | 7.30 | 15.08 | -51.59 | 8.50 | 10.54 | -19.38 |
| December 1979 | 1st Q 1980 | 13.14 | 16.40 | -19.86 | 10.57 | 12.14 | -12.96 |
| | 2nd Q 1980 | 11.79 | 16.32 | -27.77 | 10.39 | 11.20 | -7.26 |
| | 3rd Q 1980 | 11.53 | 11.61 | -0.69 | 10.43 | 11.58 | -9.90 |
| | 4th Q 1980 | 10.99 | 16.73 | -34.32 | 10.33 | 12.83 | -19.49 |
| December 1980 | 1st Q 1981 | 14.74 | 19.21 | -23.28 | 12.60 | 13.16 | -4.28 |
| | 2nd Q 1981 | 13.32 | 18.93 | -29.64 | 12.19 | 13.98 | -12.82 |
| | 3rd Q 1981 | 13.68 | 20.32 | -32.69 | 12.16 | 14.92 | -18.50 |
| | 4th Q 1981 | 13.93 | 17.01 | -18.12 | 12.23 | 14.62 | -16.33 |
| December 1981 | 1st Q 1982 | 12.57 | 16.27 | -22.74 | 14.32 | 15.01 | -4.60 |
| | 2nd Q 1982 | 12.53 | 16.50 | -24.06 | 13.55 | 14.51 | -6.62 |
| | 3rd Q 1982 | 13.74 | 14.72 | -6.64 | 13.22 | 13.75 | -3.88 |
| | 4th Q 1982 | 14.27 | 11.96 | 19.35 | 13.21 | 11.88 | 11.23 |

Sources: Board of Governors of the Federal Reserve System; Federal Reserve Bank of Richmond; UCLA National Business Forecast; U.S. Department of Commerce, Bureau of Economic Analysis.

shorter-term assets. Construction loans, though subject to substantial market and credit risks compared with residential mortgages, had relatively short maturities and potentially high returns. They seemed a desirable asset to add to S&L portfolios dominated by long-term mortgages, as well as a natural extension of the traditional S&L business. With net worth diminished by rising interest rates, it seemed to the Federal Home Loan Bank Board and other S&L regulators that it would be advantageous for S&Ls to take an equity interest in such projects.

During the severe decline in real estate markets beginning in early 1980, however, construction loans could not be repaid, because the houses and other projects could not be sold or leased. Construction loans made in 1979 turned out to be a mistake. If rising interest rates and depressed real estate market conditions were to continue for long, S&Ls would have been well-advised to look for other kinds of borrowers and other earning assets. But if 1980 was to be only a brief interruption in a long-term real estate boom, it would be wiser for bank managements to continue making such loans and, in particular, to try to benefit by their established relationships with developers who had proved to be profitable customers in the past. In the spring of 1980, or even at the beginning of 1981, after interest rates had declined (see Figure 1–1 in Chapter 1), it was not unreasonable to believe that rates would continue to fall, and that real estate markets would recover. As matters turned out, those who acted on this belief made a serious mistake. It was not simply the mismatch in assets and liabilities that damaged S&Ls as interest rates rose, but the effect of such increases on the S&Ls' borrowers.

## COMMERCIAL BANK COMPARISONS

Commercial-bank balance sheets have typically been less subject to interest rate risk than those of the S&Ls, whose balance sheets have been dominated by relatively long-term residential mortgage loans. In 1913, for example, almost 60 percent of national bank assets were loans that matured in less than 90 days (Table 2–2). While current data for maturity comparisons of assets are not readily available, the dominance of long-term residential mortgages on

**TABLE 2–2**
*Loans Maturing in Less Than and More Than 90 Days (National Banks)*

| Maturing in 90 Days or Less, by Type of Loan | Amounts |
|---|---|
| *August, 1913* | |
| On demand (one or more names) | $ 252,144,881 |
| On demand, secured by stocks, bonds, etc. | 384,583,183 |
| On time (two or more names) | 1,294,695,469 |
| On time, single name, without other security | 773,791,174 |
| On time, secured by stocks, bonds, etc. | 701,409,037 |
| Secured by real estate mortgages, etc. | 21,431,413 |
| Total | 3,428,055,157 |
| *Maturing in over 90 days* | 2,594,351,440 |
| Total | 6,022,406,597 |

Source: Office of the Comptroller of the Currency, Annual Report, 1913, p. 7.

S&L balance sheets and the continued dominance of considerably shorter-term commercial loans on the balance sheets of commercial banks make this clear.[18]

## WHY WAS INTEREST RATE RISK IGNORED FOR SO LONG?

Through the 1950s, there was little, if any, discussion among bankers, regulators, and economists about the interest rate risk incurred by banks. Interest rate changes and their effects on borrowers and the economy were extensively discussed and analyzed, but the impact on banks appears to have been ignored. In contrast, interest rate risk is now considered a critical problem for banks and bank regulators. Its emergence as a problem can be traced to relatively recent institutional and market changes that have converted the old bank problem, for the most part, "solved"—of maintaining sufficient liquidity—into a new form.

The bank problem of maintaining sufficient liquidity is as old as banking itself. Deposits payable on demand or with short maturities can run off at a rate where banks would find it difficult or impossible to meet legal demands for funds because they could not quickly convert their earning assets in sufficient amounts to meet them. As noted above, commercial banks of the 19th and early 20th centuries held a substantial proportion of their assets in short-term loans (Table 2–2).[19] While the maturity match between assets and liabilities was relatively close, liquidity problems could, nevertheless, arise because management was insufficiently conservative in holding short-term assets, or simply made a mistake in calculating its needs for funds; or because depositors lost confidence in the bank.

Interest rate changes were not viewed as a cause of liquidity problems. They were, rather, an effect, in that banks suffering from insufficient liquidity would, of necessity, restrict credit and interest rates would then tend to rise.

An early 20th-century bank that could not pay its depositors as legally required would have to suspend payments and effectively close, even though the value of its assets, by any reasonable calculation, still exceeded its liabilities. Illiquidity, as distinct from insolvency, was a sufficient threat to produce the Federal Reserve System. The Federal Reserve provided a borrowing facility to assist banks in need of liquidity, and promoted other short-term markets in which banks could borrow, including the federal funds market and the market for bankers' acceptances.

The availability of markets in which needed funds could be borrowed made it no longer necessary for solvent banks with insufficient liquid assets to close, but imposed a potential cost. The cost of borrowing might be such as to substantially reduce banks' profits. In principle, interest rate increases could threaten the viability of an illiquid bank by eliminating its earnings and, in this way, reducing its net worth.

Until recently, the cost effect of illiquidity was also constrained by government intervention and market conditions. When, because of loss of confidence during banking crises, it became apparent that there would be times when extreme needs existed ("runs"), federal deposit insurance was established to reduce, if not eliminate, the likelihood of such events. The Federal Reserve, after the early 1920s, contributed by maintaining a discount rate below market rates of interest. Cooperation among banks in restricting price competition for deposits through clearing houses and county banking associations also contributed, as did the provisions of the Banking Act of 1933 that prohibited interest payments on demand deposits and imposed maximum rates on time deposits (Regulation Q).

Market conditions were also favorable. From about 1870 to 1952, with an interruption during the first two decades of the twentieth century, interest rates trended downward. (See Figure 1–2 in Chapter 1.) While banks needing liquidity would be compelled to borrow short term when rates are likely to be high, they are not likely to remain high for long in an environment in which interest rates are generally falling. The effects of periodic surges—even sharp increases due to "crises" or business expansions—on the cost of borrowed funds and the net worth of banks are likely to be transitory.

The conditions—under which the old "illiquidity" concerns had been transformed into a "cost of borrowing" problem, which, in turn, had been adequately constrained—permitted banks to acquire longer-term assets and reduce their capital ratios. (These developments are discussed in detail in Chapter 3.) They began to break down in the early post–World War II period. Restrictions on deposit competition eroded existing constraints, which meant that banks could suffer large outflows of funds, not because of loss of confidence, but because they failed to meet market rates of interest. Further, from the early 1950s on, interest rates trended upward. Banks found they were faced with continually higher costs to hold deposits and/or for borrowing. The effects of interest rate increases on bank net worth, either by paying or not paying market rates of interest and/or as a result of a changing market valuation of their assets and liabilities, could, at least in principle, no longer be considered transitory and ignored by bank regulators. The establishment of federal deposit insurance, which had helped constrain borrowing costs, also gave taxpayers a contingent liability in cases of bank failures. By the 1980s, it was clear that bank regulators had to be alert to changes in bank net worth in response to interest rate changes.

## CONCLUSIONS

Until the last 20 years or so, interest rate risk was not a serious bank or public policy problem. It emerged as a problem out of government intervention and market developments that converted the old difficulty that banks had of maintaining sufficient liquidity into a "cost of borrowing" problem. Borrowing costs were initially constrained, but the constraints have been relaxed over the last several decades by a secular rise in interest rates and an intensification of competition in deposit markets.

From the banks' point of view, interest rate risk must now be dealt with like other risks. From a public policy point of view, bank supervisors must be alert to changes in bank net worth resulting from changes in interest rates.

## NOTES

1. This statement needs to be qualified. It appears that the Federal Reserve became concerned about the effects of interest rate increases on banks in the 1920s after it began to use open market operations to impose restraint and, to make the restraint effective, restricted access to the discount window. The Federal Reserve explicitly encouraged banks in the 1950s to hold short-term Treasury securities as a secondary reserve that could be sold to obtain funds during periods of rising interest rates and deposit withdrawals.

2. Philip Cagan provides an interesting review of the problems that developed during a period of declining interest rates, as the federal government debt, on which national bank notes were based, also declined. See "The First Fifty Years of the National Banking System—An Historical Appraisal," in *Banking and Monetary Studies,* ed. Deane Carson, Richard D. Irwin, Burr Ridge, IL, 1963.

3. The House Banking Committee that recommended a bill to establish the Federal Reserve in 1913 described the seriousness with which the seasonal interest rate problems were viewed. Report of the House Banking and Currency Committee, *Changes in the Banking and Currency System of the United States,* Report No. 69, September 9, 1913, p. 5.

4. Monthly interest rate data are from Frederick R. Macaulay, *The Movement of Interest Rates, Bond Yields and Stock Prices in the United States Since 1856,* National Bureau of Economic Research, New York, 1938, Appendix Table 10.

5. Crisis interest rate behavior reemerged at the bottom of the Great Depression. For example, commercial paper rates fell from their 1929 high of 6.25 percent to 1.38 percent in the week ending March 4, 1933. The banks were then closed during the "Bank Holiday." After the banks reopened, commercial paper rates rose sharply to 4.25 percent. Weekly interest rate data are available from the Federal Reserve Board's *Banking & Monetary Statistics, 1914–1941*.

6. A description of the efforts can be found in Irving Fisher's *Stable Money: A History of the Movement*, Adelphi Company, New York, 1934. The Stable Money Association advocated that price stability be legally made the sole objective of Federal Reserve policy. While important policy makers in the Federal Reserve, such as Benjamin Strong, Governor of the New York Reserve Bank, didn't disagree with the objective, they opposed legislation establishing such a "rule."

7. The statement by John R. Commons is from a paper titled "The Stabilization of Prices and Business," presented at the Annual Meeting of the American Economic Association in Chicago in 1924. It was published in the *American Economic Review*, vol. 15, 1925, p. 51. An interesting comment is provided by W. F. Gephart, in a "discussion" of the Commons paper published in the same volume, pp. 67–68.

8. Strictly speaking, the Federal Reserve managed "borrowed reserves," that is, borrowing from the Federal Reserve's discount window. To tighten, it would sell securities which, other things equal, would cause banks to lose reserves and borrow at the discount window. To ease, it purchased securities, which added reserves to the banking system and permitted banks to pay off their borrowing. By managing "borrowed reserves," the Fed also managed short-term interest rates. Short-term rates increased in periods of expansion and fell during contractions. In 1921, rates on 3- to 6-month Treasury notes and certificates averaged close to 5 percent. They fluctuated between 2 and 5 percent until the middle of 1927. Short-term rates began rising after midyear in 1927, and 3- to 6-month Treasury notes reached about 4.5 percent around the time of the "Crash" in October of 1929. Rates on long-term bonds declined through most of the 1920s. U.S. government bonds were less than 3.5 percent, and Aaa corporate bonds were a little over 4.5 percent in 1927. In 1928 and 1929 long-term rates rose somewhat, but government bonds were still less than 4 percent and Aaa corporate less than 5 percent in October of 1929. In 1928 and 1929, the yield curve was inverted.

9. This statement can be found in Keynes, *General Theory of Interest, Income and Employment*, Harcourt, Brace & Co., New York, 1936, p. 323. Relevant analysis can be found on pp. 80 ff. and in Chapter 17.

10. The issue is discussed by Hansen in *The American Economy*, McGraw Hill, New York, 1957, p. 52.

11. This statement is by Ervin Miller, in an article entitled "Monetary Policy in a Changing World," *Quarterly Journal of Economics*, February 1956, p. 23.

12. Hansen, *The American Economy*, 1957, p. 54.

13. Robert Roosa's influential article was entitled "Interest Rates and the Central Bank," in *Money, Trade and Economic Growth: Essays in Honor of J. H. Williams*, Macmillan, New York, 1951. The statement quoted is on p. 281. In comparison to the proportion of bank resources in long-term securities in 1948 noted by Roosa, Table 2–2 provides the results of a survey undertaken by the Comptroller of the Currency in 1913, and reported in his Annual Report for that year (pp. 7, 8). It was found that, at the time, about 57 percent of national bank loans matured in less than 90 days.

14. Roosa (1951), pp. 272–286.

15. Roosa (1951), pp. 273–76. Roosa was sophisticated about the shifts in the slope of the yield curve as short-term rates increased, not accepting a parallel shift as necessarily the result. He noted that Wynfield Riefler, a principal Federal Reserve economist of the 1920s, had questioned academic views on this issue. As noted in Chapter 4, a critical issue in dealing with interest rate risk involves the complexity of yield curve shifts as interest rates increase.

16. Roosa (1951), pp. 288–90 and note 29.

17. S&L deposit-like shares, despite being federally insured, were not restricted by interest rate maximums (Regulation Q) in the 1930s. Regulation Q maximums for commercial banks were set at 2.5 percent in January 1935 and remained unchanged through 1956. They were raised for the first time in 1957 as the result of post–World War II competition for deposit funds with S&Ls.

18. At the end of 1988, loans with maturities of less than a year were about 41 percent of bank assets, and 82 percent of bank loans. Data on the maturity of bank assets for earlier years are not readily available.

19. The dominant banking theory of the early 19th century held that banks should confine themselves to short-term commercial paper, or "real bills." These assets had maturities of 30 to 90 days. The theory had its roots in experience with attempts to hold less liquid assets, such as real estate and mortgages.

*Chapter Three*

# Capital Requirements and Interest Rate Risk: The Response of Public Policy

Twenty-five years ago, the evaluation of the capital adequacy of commercial banks by bank supervisors was viewed by many bankers and economists as a marginal exercise at best. In 1973, George Vojta, then vice president for corporate planning at Citibank, could reasonably state that "[c]urrently regulatory opinion is deeply divided on the issue of capital adequacy," that "[t]he weight of scholarly research is overwhelmingly to the effect that the level of bank capital has not been a material factor in preventing bank insolvency, and that ratio 'tests' for capital adequacy have not been useful in assessing or predicting the capability of a bank to remain solvent."[1] Today, in contrast, law and regulation have fully accepted the level of bank capital as a "material factor in preventing bank insolvencies." Capital requirements, as expressed in ratios of one kind or another, have become the single most important regulatory tool for the federal banking agencies.

The resuscitation of capital requirements over the last 15 years has been characterized by an adjustment for risk. It has, not surprisingly, led to the current supervisory efforts to incorporate interest rate risk into risk-adjusted requirements. In this chapter, we first review the emergence of modern capital requirements. We then describe the early efforts to integrate interest rate risk.

## THE PURPOSES OF BANK CAPITAL

Looking back from current issues to the operations of early banks in the United States, it is understandable that capital is viewed as necessary to limit the risks taken by creditors and to protect them against exploitation. Early banks made loans by issuing notes, payable on demand, that circulated as currency. Their noteholders had a number of concerns. Could the issuing bank redeem its notes in gold or silver (specie)? That is, was it liquid? If it was not, how far below par would its notes circulate? Would it have to sell assets at below book values and/or be liquidated? If the bank were to be liquidated, would its assets be sufficient to redeem the notes at face value? That is, was the bank solvent? Capital seemingly provided a margin of safety against losses that the bank creditors might otherwise incur.

Capital further assured creditors that the owners of the bank had a stake in its continued success as a going concern. Commercial banks were organized under corporate charters before there were general incorporation laws in the United States. As corporations, they were provided with limited liability. But in many states, and under the National Banking Act, stockholders were made liable for losses in an amount equal to the book value of their stock; that is, they had a "double liability." Such provisions, it was believed, would give owners a strong incentive to avoid excessive risks.[2]

This view of capital ties it closely to current analysis of the need to protect creditors and, today, the federal insurance funds. Historically, however, state and federal law specified only minimum levels of capital that banks had to have to be chartered. The New York General Banking Law of 1838 that provided for "free banking" required that each bank chartered must have capital stock of not less than $100,000. The National Banking Act (1863–64), based in large part on the New York law, established a minimum capital requirement of $50,000 for newly chartered banks in cities with populations of less than 10,000 and $100,000 for those in larger cities. Both federal and state laws have capital requirements for new branches. For many years, these requirements were never altered and became insignificant as a protection for creditors as banks grew in size.

They did, however, have a different significance, even though specified in absolute dollar amounts, not relative to either deposits or assets. The capital served to collateralize the notes that the banks issued to borrowers and, simultaneously, to create a market for government securities. The New York law contemplated that each "free bank's" capital would be used to purchase state securities that would be deposited with the State Comptroller, who would then issue bank notes that could circulate as currency. Under the National Banking Act, each bank, before beginning business, was required to deliver interest-bearing federal government bonds in amount no less than one-third (later one-fourth) and no more than 100 percent of its paid-in capital to the Treasurer of the United States. The Comptroller of the Currency would then issue engraved bank notes with the name of the issuing bank.[3]

In the 19th and early 20th centuries, the legal requirements were consistent with the purpose of collateralizing bank notes and channeling financial resources to the government but were of dubious value in protecting depositors, other creditors, and borrowers. Nevertheless, as discussed below, government as well as other customers have had an interest in reducing the risks of bank insolvency. Capital standards and guidelines emerged out of regulation and supervision, and ultimately, requirements have been imposed by law.

## THE SECULAR DECLINE IN BANK CAPITAL RATIOS

Viewing bank capital as a protection against losses that can result in insolvency, the amount in any bank must be defined in relative terms—that is, as a ratio to the assets and/or liabilities which generate the risk of insolvency. The balance sheet items used to evaluate capital can be organized in a variety of ways, with the levels of specific ratios varying accordingly. For example, "capital" can be defined narrowly to include only equity, retained earnings, and surplus, or more broadly to include certain reserves and long-term subordinated debt. Ratios can be developed on the basis of deposits or assets, of one kind or another. The rapid expansion of deposits, relative to bank notes, in the 19th and early 20th centuries led to assessments of capital-to-deposit ratios, since it was the volatility of deposits that seemed the principal threat; in the panics of the late 19th century, it was depositors that placed pressure on banks by converting, en masse, to currency. After the Federal Reserve was established and began operating to moderate deposit volatility, it became apparent that default or credit risk was more important, and that capital should be measured relative to assets rather than to deposits. It further became clear, during World War II, when banks acquired large amounts of default risk–free government securities, that not all assets were equally risky and that some measure of "risk assets" rather than total assets should be the standard against which capital was evaluated.

Overwhelming any differences in definition of balance sheet items or ratios, however, has been the decline in bank capital through the 19th century and most of the 20th. Put another way, bank leverage has, over most of the 200-year history of the United States, been increasing.

The early high capital ratios and their subsequent decline are shown in Table 3–1. In Massachusetts, a state in which well-established banks developed early, the ratio of total capital to total assets was about 73 percent in 1805. By 1835, it had declined to 54 percent; and in 1860, it was 48.5 percent.

The decline in capital ratios continued after passage of the National Banking Act. In the "all bank" series that is dominated by commercial banks, the total capital–to–total asset ratio in 1860 was about 42 percent. By 1900, it had dropped to 18 percent. In 1929, it was 13.6 percent.

Capital as a percentage of assets in the banking industry continued to decline during the Great Depression and World War II. At the end of the war, it was just a little over 6 percent. Thereafter, until 1970, the ratios fluctuated in the 6 to 8 percent range.

The causes of the secular decline in capital ratios are not completely clear. It is plausible that the decline reflects changes in the economic and regulatory environment. Early banks, without a track record, and with only ad hoc and uncertain government regulation, supervision, and support, would probably have required high levels of capital to attract creditors. As states began to exercise greater regulatory authority, banks probably found that the minimum ratios they had established for their own business purposes could be lowered as market opportunities to increase profits presented themselves. Further, passage of the National Banking Act, with its collateralized currency, and subsequently the Federal Reserve Act in 1913, may also have contributed to the sense of creditors that they were protected by special government provisions, as well as by bank capital.

**TABLE 3–1**
*Ratio of Capital to Assets, Massachusetts and All Banks, 1805–1970 (%)*

| Year | Massachusetts Banks | All Banks |
|------|---------------------|-----------|
| 1805 | 73.3 | |
| 1810 | 60.4 | |
| 1815 | 77.7 | |
| 1820 | 63.9 | |
| 1825 | 57.5 | |
| 1830 | 51.7 | |
| 1835 | 54.1 | 46.4 |
| 1840 | 58.8 | 54.4 |
| 1845 | 47.7 | 47.5 |
| 1850 | 48.7 | 40.1 |
| 1855 | 50.1 | 40.1 |
| 1860 | 48.5 | 42.2 |
| 1865 | | 33.3 |
| 1870 | | 36.4 |
| 1875 | | 26.4 |
| 1880 | | 24.3 |
| 1885 | | 23.5 |
| 1890 | | 24.5 |
| 1895 | | 23.4 |
| 1900 | | 18.2 |
| 1905 | | 17.5 |
| 1910 | | 17.4 |
| 1915 | | 16.4 |
| 1920 | | 11.3 |
| 1925 | | 11.9 |
| 1930 | | 13.4 |
| 1935 | | 13.0 |
| 1940 | | 10.4 |
| 1945 | | 6.2 |
| 1950 | | 7.8 |
| 1955 | | 7.7 |
| 1960 | | 8.4 |
| 1965 | | 8.3 |
| 1970 | | 7.8 |

Notes: The "all banks" series includes commercial banks, trust companies, and savings institutions.

Sources: Massachusetts banks, Annual Report of the Comptroller of the Currency, 1876, pp. 98, 99; all banks, Historical Statistics of the United States, U.S. Department of Commerce, Part II, 1976, Ch. X, p. 1019.

The declining capital-to-asset ratios in the late 19th and early 20th centuries may also reflect the expansion of deposit banking in the United States. Under the National Banking Act, it was advantageous for banks to have high levels of capital in order to secure large volumes of national bank notes. But by the 1880s, national banks found that they could operate with deposits and without bank notes, and therefore could afford to let capital ratios decline.[4] With the development of secondary markets for government bonds after the Civil War, and the establishment of the Federal Reserve System in 1914 as a support, the federal government's need to tie banks tightly to its fiscal needs through their capital accounts also diminished.

The decline in capital ratios during and for some years following World War II may be attributable to the acquisition by banks of large volumes of default-free government securities. The further decline in capital ratios during and following the Great Depression has sometimes been attributed to the new protections afforded bank creditors by the regulatory reforms of the 1930s. Federal deposit insurance, the imposition of legal restrictions on "price" competition for deposits and informal restrictions on competition in general, and constraints on seemingly "risky" activities like underwriting securities appear to have reduced the perceived as well as the actual likelihood of bank failure. Between 1943 and 1970, the number of bank failures never exceeded 9 in any one year and was typically 5 or less.

With deregulation in recent years and an intensification of competition, it has been argued that the existence of a federal "safety net"—that is, the discount window, the Fedwire, deposit insurance, and "too-big-to-fail" assurances—by imposing a contingent liability on taxpayers, provides banks with a substitute for capital. Several years ago, in an address to bankers and economists, Alan Greenspan, Federal Reserve Board Chairman, looked back to the capital ratios of the 1840s and the 1920s and observed that "pure market economy banks are . . . forced to maintain substantial capital to attract funds." He then provided the rationale for legal and/or regulatory requirements that are higher than banks would establish on their own. "We might also consider the desirability of returning to capital requirements that more closely simulate those that the market dictated in a world without a safety net."[5]

# THE TRADITIONAL REGULATORY
# EVALUATION OF CAPITAL

As noted, capital requirements for newly organized banks have long been imposed by law in the United States. Ongoing evaluations of bank capital for safety and soundness were left to regulators who dealt with each bank on an individual basis. Prior to the passage of recent laws (FIRREA and FDICIA), the regulatory agencies drew on their general authority to supervise banks as a basis for evaluating bank capital positions and their adequacy. For example, the Federal Reserve's authority emerges from Section 9 of the Federal Reserve Act, which requires that the capital and surplus of a member bank "shall be adequate in relation to the character and condition of its assets and to its deposit liabilities and other corporate responsibilities." Nonmember insured banks have been required to maintain "adequate capital" as a condition of deposit insurance. The specification of terms such as "adequate in relation to the character and condition of its assets" was left to supervisory discretion, and implementation was left to supervisory-bank negotiations.

While banking laws provided general authority for regulators to appraise the capital adequacy of banks, they gave little specific guidance to how that was to be done and to what purposes. As a result, individual agencies altered their approaches over time, independently of one another. At any one time, the approaches of the three principal federal commercial banking agencies (the Comptroller of the Currency, the Federal Reserve, and the FDIC) were likely to be strikingly different. The agencies, moreover, could not agree on the definition of "capital" itself. The Federal Reserve, for example, had traditionally focused on equity, while the FDIC had a broader definition that included some debt instruments. The Federal Home Loan Bank Board, the federal regulator for S&Ls prior to 1989, had a completely independent design, requiring minimum ratios of capital to deposits and including in capital large amounts of "supervisory goodwill" and other intangible elements.

A brief review of how supervisory views and strategies have changed over the years helps place current approaches in perspective. In the early 1860s, the Comptroller of the Currency believed that national banks had too much capital.[6] In 1914, the Comptroller had altered his views, and suggested that "it is not sound banking for an active commercial bank to be allowed to receive deposits in excess of ten times its capital and surplus.[7] In the 1960s, as discussed in more detail below, the Comptroller decided that formal ratios were too inaccurate a measure of capital to be useful.

As noted, in the late 1930s, the federal regulatory agencies began to focus on ratios of capital to assets rather than capital to deposits. By the early 1950s, the Federal Reserve was suggesting that, at a minimum, this ratio should be 7 percent. The FDIC, on the other hand, used the national average of the ratio as the standard, criticizing banks in accordance with how far they fell below the average.

The change from deposits to assets as the denominator for the capital ratio necessitated a consideration of the various kinds of assets that banks held. As banks increased their holdings of government securities during World War II, it became clear that, for capital evaluations, distinctions had to be made between relatively risky and less risky assets. The regulatory focus shifted from total assets to a rough measure of risk assets that excluded cash, bank balances, and government securities. The early efforts to establish "risk-adjusted" capital ratios can, then, be traced to the banking developments of World War II.

In the early 1950s, the Federal Reserve pushed the rough risk-asset ratio further, by establishing a minimum capital standard of 20 percent of a bank's risk assets, that is, $1 of capital for $5 of risk assets. Subsequently, it attempted to categorize all assets according to risk and to assign differing capital requirements to each category. It added off–balance sheet items to the analysis and introduced a liquidity test, requiring more capital from banks that were less liquid.[8]

The Comptroller of the Currency, on the other hand, was suspicious of ratio analysis. In September 1962, his Advisory Committee on Banking, reflecting a long-held view of the American Bankers Association, stated that the arbitrary formulas which had been followed in the past did not provide a reasonable basis for determining capital adequacy, and cited a number of other factors that needed to be considered, including the quality of management, the earnings record of the bank, volatility of deposits, audit procedures, and the economic characteristics of the bank's trade area. In December 1962, the Comptroller indicated agreement and that he would follow the recommendations of the Committee. In the late 1960s, the Comptroller amended national bank regulations accordingly.

## INCREASING CONCERN ABOUT DECLINING RATIOS IN THE 1970s

Whatever the reasons underlying the long-term decline in bank capital ratios, further decline in the 1970s generated considerable concern among bank regulators as they were accompanied by failures of some large banking organizations. Total equity capital-to-assets for all insured commercial banks was 6.8 percent in 1970 (Table 3–2). By 1979, it had dropped to 5.8 percent. The ratios for large banks fell even more. In 1970, the capital-to-asset ratio for banks with $1 billion or more in assets had been 5.9 percent. By 1976, it had declined to 4.9 percent. And by 1979, it was 4.6 percent. The average ratio for money center banks in 1980 was 3.9 percent.

The federal regulatory agencies were well aware of the long-term trends, and in particular of the post–World War II developments. But during the 1950s and 1960s they found little reason to intervene inasmuch as the numbers of bank failures were minuscule. And the failures that did occur were, almost invariably, small banks that ran into problems because of mismanagement or fraud, not insufficient capital levels. It was, indeed, plausible that the crude capital ratios that had been utilized were of little value.

The problem banks of the 1970s, while not large in number, included a number of large banks. In 1972, the FDIC found it necessary to assist the Bank of the Commonwealth, a Detroit organization with $1.3 billion in assets, to keep it from failing. In 1973, the U.S. National Bank of San Diego, also with about $1.3 billion in assets, failed. And in 1974, Franklin National of New York, with close to $4 billion in assets, had to be closed. Seventeen cases of failure and/or assistance to prevent failure in 1976, including the old and well-established Hamilton National Bank of Chattanooga, were more than had occurred in any year since 1942. In 1980, the First Pennsylvania Bank, with close to $8 billion in assets, was assisted by the FDIC to prevent failure.[9]

**TABLE 3–2**
*Capital/Assets Ratio for All Insured Commercial Banks by Consolidated Asset Size, End of Period*
*(Average Equity to Average Assets, %)*

|  | 1970 | 1971 | 1972 | 1973 | 1974 | 1975 | 1976 | 1977 | 1978 | 1979 | 1980 | 1981 |
|---|---|---|---|---|---|---|---|---|---|---|---|---|
| All insured banks | 6.8 | 6.5 | 6.2 | 5.9 | 5.7 | 5.9 | 6.1 | 6.0 | 5.9 | 5.8 | 5.8 | 5.8 |
| Banks with: |  |  |  |  |  |  |  |  |  |  |  |  |
| Less than $100 million | 7.8 | 7.7 | 7.5 | 7.4 | 7.6 | 7.8 | 7.9 | 7.9 | 7.9 | 8.1 | 8.4 | 8.5 |
| $100 million to $1 billion | 7.4 | 7.1 | 6.0 | 6.6 | 6.7 | 6.8 | 7.0 | 6.9 | 6.8 | 6.9 | 7.0 | 7.1 |
| $1 billion and over | 5.9 | 5.5 | 5.2 | 4.9 | 4.4 | 4.6 | 4.9 | 4.9 | 4.8 | 4.6 | 4.6 | 4.6 |
| Money center | 5.8 | 5.4 | 5.1 | 4.6 | 4.0 | 4.1 | 4.4 | 4.3 | 4.2 | 4.0 | 3.9 | 3.9 |
| Other | 6.0 | 5.7 | 5.3 | 5.2 | 4.9 | 5.3 | 5.6 | 5.6 | 5.4 | 5.3 | 5.2 | 5.3 |

Based upon the average of beginning and end of year of fully consolidated assets net of loan loss reserves. Money centers: Bank of America, Bankers Trust, Chase Manhattan, Chemical, Citibank, Continental Illinois, First Chicago, First National Boston, Harris Trust, Manufacturers Hanover, Mellon, Morgan Guaranty, Northern Trust.

Source: *Recent Trends in Commercial Bank Profitability*, Federal Reserve Bank of New York, September 1986, p. 15.

During the 1970s, the Federal Reserve was more or less distinguished by its efforts to impose higher levels of capital on banks and bank holding companies. In 1972, it revised its ABC forms to what George Vojta, in his monograph *Bank Capital Adequacy,* termed "a more conservative extreme." Among other things, it separated asset risk factors into credit risk and market risk, an early recognition of the interest rate risk problems that were to develop at the end of the decade. In 1974, Arthur Burns, Chairman of the Federal Reserve Board, indicated that he did not believe bank capital was adequate. The Federal Reserve, focusing on the financial condition of bank holding companies, undertook a "go slow" policy in permitting their entry into new activities. Burns explained in oversight hearings before the Senate Committee on Banking in March of 1977:

> Individual companies have been allowed to expand into new areas only when the Board has been satisfied with their financial condition and managerial capabilities. On the other hand, companies whose asset composition, capital or liquidity raises doubts, ought by now to know that the Board will be extremely skeptical of proposals that divert financial or managerial resources to new undertakings. . . . Moreover, in some instances in which applications for expansion have been approved, the authority to proceed has been made conditional on improvement of the applicant's capital base. The Board intends to continue using such leverage in the interest of assuring further improvement in the condition of the banking system.

## NEW CAPITAL REQUIREMENTS IN THE EARLY 1980s

George Vojta, as noted, observed in the early 1970s that "regulatory opinion is deeply divided on the issue of capital adequacy." Bankers and economists criticized the Federal Reserve severely for using its authority under the Bank Holding Company Act to obtain compliance with capital standards on which other supervisory agencies did not agree.[10] At the time, it was not unusual for a banking organization, supervised by multiple regulators, to confront conflicting judgments on the need for additional capital. In the case, for example, of a state-chartered Federal Reserve member bank, the state supervisor and the Federal Reserve might have sharply different views as to how much capital was needed.

By the end of the 1970s, however, the combination of declining capital ratios, particularly at large banks, the failure of "large" banks, and perhaps the damage incurred by S&Ls during the early 1980s led all the federal commercial banking agencies to reconsider their positions on capital requirements. The failure of several important holding companies in the 1970s, including Hamilton Bancshares in 1974, Beverly Hills Bancorp in 1973, and Palmer Bancorporation in 1975, had already driven them to the realization that they could not effectively supervise one or even several affiliates in a holding company without authority over the entire organization. The further implication was that overlapping authority that resulted in conflicting proscriptions was disastrous.

The new banking agency interest in coordination and capital requirements may also have been motivated by a better understanding of the effects of low capital ratios on bank behavior. While capital had long been viewed as a protection against insolvency and the "double liability" provisions of earlier banking law were aimed at further protecting creditors, the effects of low levels of capital on the willingness of banks to take excessive risk had not been completely clear. In the late 1970s, new theoretical analysis had indicated that banks supported by federal deposit insurance with premiums unadjusted for risk were likely to take excessive risks; the federal safety net subsidized risk taking and created a moral hazard by providing a substitute for equity capital.[11] Models of firms near bankruptcy implied that low levels of capital, independently of deposit insurance, encouraged firms to take excessive risks.[12] Later empirical analysis of insolvency and risk taking in the thrift industry supported the earlier theoretical work on the relationship between low levels of capital and "moral hazard."[13]

In 1980, there were no capital requirements in the same sense as, for example, there were "reserve requirements" for Federal Reserve member banks. Agencies imposed their own, individual standards on a bank-by-bank basis. In 1981, however, the OCC and the Federal Reserve announced a common set of capital standards that would apply to all national and other member banks and all bank holding companies. At the same time, the FDIC announced a somewhat different set of requirements. It was not until March of 1985 that the FDIC adopted the requirements of the other two federal agencies.

The 1981 announcement involved the issuance of "capital guidelines" that effectively imposed minimums designed to increase bank capital. Under the arrangement, capital was divided into "primary" and "secondary" components. Primary capital included such elements as common and perpetual preferred stock, allocated capital reserves, mandatory convertible instruments, and allowances for loan losses. Secondary capital included limited-life preferred stock and longer-term subordinated notes and debentures, among other elements. Total capital was defined as the sum of primary and secondary elements.

The guidelines divided banks into three groups: (1) multinational organizations (as a practical matter, this group included the 17 largest banking organizations), (2) regional organizations with assets over $1 billion, and (3) community banks with assets less than $1 billion. No numerical standards were set initially for the multinational organizations, but regulators made clear that they expected them to improve their capital positions.[14] A minimum ratio of primary capital to assets was established at 5 percent for regional organizations and 6 percent for community banks; and respectively, 6.5 percent and 7 percent for total capital to assets.

As can be seen in Table 3–3, capital ratios began to increase in the early 1980s. The average ratio for all insured commercial banks rose from 5.8 percent in 1981 to 6.2 percent by 1985. There has been some academic dispute as to whether these increases were due to regulatory requirements or market pressures that would have resulted in increases regardless of requirements.[15]

## RISK-ADJUSTED RATIOS

Despite the improvements in capital ratios, by the mid-1980s at least two factors were pushing the federal banking agencies toward a further revision of capital standards so as to make adjustments for the risks banks incurred. First, they perceived that banks could avoid the costly impact of the higher standards that had been set by accepting greater portfolio risk, and by increasing their off–balance sheet activities, such as standby letters of credit, that were not included in calculating the minimum "leverage ratios" that had been established.[16] Second, no progress had been made in

**TABLE 3–3**
*Equity Capital and Assets: All Insured Commercial Banks*
*December 31, 1981, to December 31, 1992 ($ Millions)*

| Year | Total Equity | Total Assets | Equity to Assets |
|------|-------------|-------------|-----------------|
| 1981 | $118,241 | $2,029,150 | 5.8% |
| 1982 | 128,698 | 2,193,867 | 5.9 |
| 1983 | 140,459 | 2,341,952 | 6.0 |
| 1984 | 154,103 | 2,508,871 | 6.1 |
| 1985 | 169,118 | 2,730,672 | 6.2 |
| 1986 | 182,144 | 2,940,699 | 6.2 |
| 1987 | 180,651 | 2,999,949 | 6.0 |
| 1988 | 196,546 | 3,130,796 | 6.3 |
| 1989 | 204,823 | 3,299,363 | 6.2 |
| 1990 | 218,623 | 3,389,471 | 6.5 |
| 1991 | 231,711 | 3,430,576 | 6.8 |
| 1992 | 263,560 | 3,505,961 | 7.5 |
| 1993 | 296,523 | 3,706,189 | 8.0 |
| 1994 | 312,187 | 4,010,664 | 7.8 |

Source: FDIC, *Historical Statistics on Banking: 1934–1992*, September 1993, Table CB-17, p. 102; and FDIC, *Quarterly Banking Profile: Fourth Quarter, 1994*, p. 15.

adjusting deposit insurance premiums for risk. In fact, the insolvency of Continental Illinois National Bank in 1984 resulted in an FDIC rescue that included support not simply of insured depositors of the bank but of all creditors of the holding company. The Continental case appeared to reaffirm the market perception that creditors of large banks were providing "risk-free" funds, in part, because the federal agencies would not permit large banks to fail. The behavior of the regulators in the Continental case augmented concerns that risk taking was subsidized by the federal "safety net" so that a serious "moral hazard" was being generated.

With an intent to offset the risk-taking incentives in simple leverage requirements, the Federal Reserve began working on risk-based capital standards in the summer of 1985. The Office of the Comptroller of the Currency took the position that the "risk-based capital approach is preferable to relying on risk-based insurance premiums."[17] In September, Paul Volker, then Chairman of the Board, told the Senate Banking Committee what the Board had in mind. A month later, in an address to the annual convention of the American Bankers Association, he indicated that the Board had "been looking at the feasibility of supplementing (but not replacing) the current guidelines with a risk-based measure, in effect providing a 'second opinion' on capital adequacy."

In early 1986, the Federal Reserve proposed a new set of risk-based capital requirements, and the Comptroller of the Currency and the FDIC indicated that their intent was to join in modifying their own requirements to adjust for risk. The Fed's proposal reshuffled the elements of capital into new categories once more. "Core capital" (Tier 1) was intended to be more restrictive than "primary capital" in the older system. It was to include only permanent shareholder equity, retained earnings, and surplus. It included common equity, and qualified perpetual preferred stock. It excluded "goodwill." "Supplementary capital" (Tier 2) was to include, among other elements, subordinated debt, allowances for loan losses, and long-term preferred stock. The sum of "core" and "supplementary" capital was designated "total capital."

A risk-adjusted ratio was developed by creating four categories of assets with varying risks, and assigning a percentage risk weight to each. At one extreme, "cash and its equivalents," including short-term Treasury securities, were assigned a zero weight—in effect, they required no capital. At the other extreme, assets in a bank's loan portfolio carried a 100 percent weight—the full amount of capital indicated by the minimum ratio would be required. Loans sold with recourse, that no longer appeared on the books, carried a 100 percent weight. In between short-term Treasuries and loans, "money market risk" assets and "moderate risk assets" were assigned a 30 percent and 60 percent weight, respectively. A required minimum ratio of total capital to risk-weighted assets and core capital to risk-weighted assets was established. The initial plan proposed a minimum ratio of core capital to risk-weighted assets of 7.5 percent.

There were a number of disagreements among the regulators in the development of this system. The FDIC had indicated an intention to retain the older primary and total capital ratios. The OCC viewed "top-rated banks" somewhat differently than the Federal Reserve and the FDIC. A key problem that each of the agencies confronted was that the risk-adjusted system did not apply to foreign banks with whom U.S. banks competed.

In the fall of 1986, the agencies deferred implementation of their plans in favor of work with the Bank of England and subsequently other countries to develop common international standards for evaluating capital. In January 1987, a joint U.S.–UK (Bank of England) proposal was issued. By July, a broader agreement for a new a "risk-adjusted" system was reflected in a proposal by the Basle Committee on Bank Regulations and Supervision (Basle Committee) that included central banks and bank regulators of the Group of 10 (G10) countries, plus Switzerland and Luxembourg.

A final accord was reached in June 1988. The accord was for an interim minimum ratio beginning January 1, 1991, of 7.25 percent for total capital to risk based assets, and 3.25 percent for core capital to risk based assets. Minimum standards of 8 percent and 4 percent, respectively, were to be established on January 1, 1993.

The Financial Institutions Reform, Recovery and Enforcement Act (FIRREA), passed in August 1989, incorporated thrifts into the new arrangement. It required that the Office of Thrift Supervision (OTS) impose risk-based capital standards no less stringent than those applicable to national banks.

As discussed in Chapter 1, minimum risk-adjusted capital ratios established by regulation have been required by the passage of FDICIA. They have been closely tied to "prompt corrective action" that specifies the type and nature of regulatory intervention that will occur if they are not met. Bank capital ratios, however, have risen in recent years so that relatively few have not reached the mandated standards on both a leverage and risk-adjusted basis. The vast majority of banks have, in recent years, exceeded standards. By the end of 1994, over 98 percent were classified as "well capitalized." [18]

## INTEREST RATE RISK AND CAPITAL REQUIREMENTS

The Federal Banking Agency proposals in 1986 and the Basle proposal of 1987 focused almost exclusively on credit risk. It was recognized that there were other risks for which bank capital was required, including foreign exchange risk, liquidity risk, and interest rate risk. The interest rate risk issue was apparently one of the more controversial ones raised in the Basle negotiations. At the time of the accord, the Federal Reserve indicated that it would consider incorporating an interest rate risk component before the new risk-adjusted system went into effect in 1991.[19]

As with other issues on which agreement is not feasible, a typical strategy is to subject it to further study. This is what has occurred on an international level. The Basle Committee declared an intention to develop a measurement system rather than an explicit capital charge in April 1993. The general philosophy was that: . . . "a certain degree of interest rate mismatching is a normal feature of the business of banking," and "existing capital requirements can be regarded as providing adequate protection against interest rate risk exposure in most situations. The measurement system is designed to identify institutions that may be incurring extraordinarily large amounts of interest rate risk. . . . The range of responses by national authorities might include an explicit capital charge on a case-by-case basis, but the situation could also be dealt with by a number of other supervisory remedies." . . .[20]

In April of 1995, the Basle Committee issued a proposal to amend the 1988 accord to incorporate market risks for foreign exchange, commodities, and trading activities of large international banks. The committee's proposal stated that the committee

> plans to revert to the question of interest rate risk at a later date. In the meantime, its members will continue to use national methods to measure the interest rate risk in the whole bank and, in so doing, to learn from the experience of their colleagues in this respect. It is hoped that the experience gathered from the implementation of the market risk package will provide useful guidance in progressing the debate on appropriate ways of measuring interest rate risk.[21]

The interest rate risk issue has had a more or less unique development in the United States. The experience of the early 1980s made clear, if it were not clear long before, that S&Ls were vulnerable in the extreme. The Federal Home Loan Bank Board, however, did not initially take the impact of volatile rates on S&Ls as an indication that capital requirements needed to be adjusted upward. In fact, in contrast to the commercial banking regulators, it lowered capital requirements in 1982, reducing the minimum net worth requirement from 4 percent of liabilities to 3 percent. In addition, it included a number of elements in capital, as noted, that diverged from Generally Accepted Accounting Principles (GAAP) and which papered over capital deficiencies.

By the mid-1980s, however, it was recognized by FHLBB regulators that interest rate risk constituted a critical threat to thrifts. In the Secondary Mortgage Market Enhancement Act of 1984, thrifts with federal deposit insurance were required to establish policies for the management of interest rate risk. From 1984 to 1989, thrifts reported interest rate risk information to the Federal Home Loan Bank Board on a confidential basis. Between 1987 and 1989, thrift net worth standards included an interest rate risk component.[22]

The practices that had been developed for thrifts, however, were terminated by passage of FIRREA in 1989. The act required that the Office of Thrift Supervision (OTS), the new regulator for S&Ls, issue risk-based capital standards comparable to those for national banks. It was contemplated that interest rate risk would be incorporated in these capital standards. In 1991, with the passage of FDICIA, the contemplation was mandated, as discussed in Chapter 2. But as yet, no final regulation imposing a specific capital charge for interest rate risk has been issued.[23]

## CONCLUSIONS

In the early 1970s, capital adequacy standards were, for the most part, informal and uncertain. The long-run decline in capital ratios was viewed as little more than an interesting characteristic that might be of some concern at some point, something like the increase in bank loan-deposit ratios in the post–World War II period. The transfiguration of capital standards from a nonbinding requirement for newly chartered banks and new branches and a relatively arbitrary and controversial supervisory tool to the principal instrument of bank regulation, incorporating highly complex and sophisticated financial analyses, has taken place since the late 1970s, over a period of about 18 years.

In the decade of the 1970s, increasing competition, large bank failures, deregulation, and a better understanding of the function of capital sparked a reevaluation of the need for legal and regulatory requirements. The implicit conclusion reached by the regulators and Congress, and the underlying assumption on which subsequent regulatory efforts have been based, is as follows: for nonregulated businesses, the market can generally be relied on to require whatever amount of capital is appropriate; for banking, however, the absence of publicly available relevant information, in a timely manner, on the condition of banks makes it difficult for financial markets to impose the necessary pressure. Moreover, the support provided banks by the federal "safety net" that puts taxpayers at risk would result in market judgments to require less capital than otherwise would be the case; it then becomes essential for minimum capital standards to be established by public authority.

Once Congress and the federal regulatory agencies decided that bank capital levels, even though falling for close to 200 years, had fallen too far, simple logic compelled the radical changes that have taken place. In the context of the modern banking institution, with a wide and growing set of potential activities, subject to competitive pressure from other firms, and with the rapid appearance of new kinds of financial instruments, minimum capital ratios that might have been acceptable in a sleepier time are insufficient. It was necessary that minimum ratios be established on a risk-adjusted basis. If the purpose was to establish a buffer to absorb the potential losses resulting from risk, then all risk, not simply credit risk, would have to be evaluated. Interest rate risk that had crippled the S&L industry in the early 1980s would clearly have to be incorporated. If banks in the United States (or any other country) were to be compelled to establish minimum risk-adjusted standards, international agreement to provide a level playing field was essential. The effort to incorporate all identified risks and integrate them into risk-adjusted capital requirements, and on an international basis, has been a monumental undertaking. There have been numerous political as well as economic issues raised. It has strained the technical expertise available. The inability to specify fully an acceptable interest rate risk element, up to now, is testimony of the difficulties involved.

Looking at this regulatory "trend," Alan Greenspan issued an ominous warning to the Conference on Bank Structure and Competition at the Federal Reserve Bank of Chicago in May 1993:

> A characteristic of the modern banking system is that technological advances breed increasing numbers of ways to take on risk, as well as increasing numbers of ways to measure and control risk. Thus, we see ever more diversity across banks in their approaches toward risk management. No single quantitative standard or ratio could capture this diversity across institutions, nor even capture the complexity of risk at any one institution. Moreover, rigidly applied formulas can not adequately take account of the need for banks to evolve; regulatory formulas may, in fact, stifle productive innovation.

The measurement of interest rate risk, and the difficulties that arise, are discussed in Chapter 4.

## NOTES

1. The statements are from Vojta's well-known monograph *Capital Adequacy* in 1973 (pp. 9 and 12). In the introduction, Walter Wriston, then chairman of First National City Bank (now Citibank), noted that "scholarly research indicates that most of the banks which have closed their doors in the past have met or exceeded capital ratio tests applied by regulators immediately prior to their bankruptcy."

2. For an interesting review of the early history of bank capital, see the remarks of Wayne D. Angell, former Federal Reserve Board Governor, before the 1992 Business Law Symposium of the Wake Forest Law Review, March 27, 1992.

3. The original provision was that the notes obtained by any one bank could not exceed $300 million and they could not be greater in amount than 90 percent of the par or market value of the bonds deposited, whichever was lower.

4. After 1880, the profitability of national bank notes declined as interest rates on government bonds fell and their market prices rose above par. Other assets provided a better return. For a calculation of the decline in profit rates on national bank notes, see Philip Cagan, "The First Fifty Years of the National Banking System—An Historical Appraisal," *Banking and Monetary Studies*, ed. Deane Carson, Richard D. Irwin, Burr Ridge, IL, 1963, p. 22.

5. These remarks were made in an address in 1990 to the Conference on Bank Structure and Competition at the Federal Reserve Bank of Chicago. The address can be found in the proceedings of the conference, pp. 1–8.

6. An interesting summary of some of the Comptroller's early views can be found in an article by Wesley Lindow, then senior vice president of the Irving Trust Company of New York, in the *National Banking Review*, September, 1963. Another useful review of earlier views on capital adequacy can be found in *Management Policies for Commercial Banks*, by Howard Crosse and George Hemple (Prentice Hall, Englewood Cliffs, NJ, 1972, Chapter 5). Crosse, a principal bank supervisor at the Federal Reserve Bank of New York, was one of the architects of the Federal Reserve's approach.

7. The Comptroller's views in 1914 can be found in the *Annual Report of the Comptroller of the Currency*, 1914, vol. 1, p. 21. At the time, the view that deposits should not be less than 10 times capital and surplus implied a capital-to-asset ratio of about 9 percent. As can be seen in Table 3–1, the average ratios for banks were well above this level in the early years of the 20th century.

8. The Federal Reserve's approach to capital adequacy can be traced from the approach first taken by the Federal Reserve Bank of New York in the early 1950s as indicated in "A Measure of Minimum Capital Adequacy," December 21, 1952, through the more complex ABC forms (forms for "Analyzing Bank Capital") of the Board of Governors in 1956 and the amendment of the latter in 1972.

9. The data on bank closings and FDIC-assisted transactions are from the FDIC, *Historical Statistics on Banking*, September 1993, Tables BC 69–81, pp. 606–618.

10. See, for example, the comment of George Vojta, footnote 18 p. 13, in *Bank Capital Adequacy*, First National City Bank, February 1973.

11. The early work on deposit insurance included J. H. Kareken and N. Wallace, "Deposit Insurance and Bank Regulation: A Partial Equilibrium Exposition," *Journal of Business*, July 1978, pp. 413–38; R. C. Merton, "On the Cost of Deposit Insurance and Security Values," *Journal of Financial and Quantitative Analysis*, July 1978, pp. 439–52; and W. F. Sharpe, "Bank Capital Adequacy, Deposit Insurance and Security Values," *Journal of Financial and Quantitative Analysis*, November 1978, pp. 701–18.

12. See, for example, Devra Golbe, "The Effects of Imminent Bankruptcy on Stockholder Risk Preferences and Behavior," *Bell Journal of Economics*, Spring 1981, pp. 321–28.

13. For example, see Devra Golbe and Bernard Shull, "Risk Taking by Thrift Institutions: A Framework for Empirical Investigation," *Contemporary Policy Issues,* vol. IX, July 1991, p. 107. The low levels of capital in the thrift industry had resulted, in part, from interest rate increases in the early 1980s, substantial loan losses thereafter, and also a regulatory policy that encouraged rapid growth as a solution to the problem.

14. In June of 1983, multinational organizations were required to meet the 5 percent minimum primary capital-to-total assets standard.

15. Larry D. Wall, in "Capital Requirements for Banks," *Economic Review,* Federal Reserve Bank of Atlanta, March–April, 1989, provides a useful review of the studies evaluating the new capital requirements of the 1980s and the evolution of the capital requirements themselves.

16. For a discussion of these developments, see Larry D. Wall's article in the *Economic Review,* Federal Reserve Bank of Atlanta, March–April, 1989, pp. 16 ff.

17. Deputy Comptroller Michael Patriarca testified before the Subcommittee on Financial Institutions of the House Banking Committee on September 11, 1985, that "[r]equiring the level of capital to be commensurate with a bank's risk would be a more direct way to encourage reasoned risk-taking, and would involve more of the marketplace—equity holders—in the process of disciplining banks."

18. For the distribution of banks in March 1995 within regulatory classifications that consider both their capital ratios and supervisor "CAMEL" ratings, and which derive from the Federal Deposit Insurance Corporation Improvement Act of 1991 (FDICIA), see Chapter 1, Table 1–3. CAMEL is the acronym for composite supervisory ratings based on a bank's capital, assets, management, earnings and liquidity.

19. The international agreement and the Fed's concern about interest rate risk are discussed by Malcom Alfriend in the *Economic Review* of the Federal Reserve Bank of Richmond, November–December 1988, pp. 30–31. See also Jeffrey Bardos, "The Risk-Based Capital Agreement: A Further Step towards Policy Convergence," *Quarterly Review,* Federal Reserve Bank of New York, Winter 1987–88, vol. 12, no. 4, p. 32. Lawrence J. White, a former member of the Federal Home Loan Bank Board, has pointed out in *The S&L Debacle* (Oxford University Press, Oxford, 1991) that the FIRREA requirement to establish risk-based capital standards for thrifts no less stringent than

those applicable to national banks precluded the OTS, at least temporarily, from establishing requirements about to go into effect when FIRREA was passed that would have included interest rate risk component (p. 187).

20. "The Prudential Supervision of Netting, Market Risks and Interest Rate Risk," Preface to Consultative Proposal by the Basle Committee on Banking Supervision, April 1993, p. 4.

21. Proposal to Issue a Supplement to the Basle Capital Accord to Cover Market Risks, Consultative Proposal by the Basle Committee on Banking Supervision, April 1995, p. 7.

22. Useful information on the regulatory behavior of the now departed Federal Home Loan Bank Board can be found in R. Dan Brumbaugh, *Thrifts under Siege,* Ballinger, Cambridge, MA, 1988. See pp. 42 and 43 in particular. Lawrence J. White has also provided useful information and insights in *The S&L Debacle,* Oxford University Press, Oxford, 1991. See, in particular, pp. 186–87, and p. 247, notes 12 and 16.

23. The OTS currently has an extensive reporting system, discussed in Chapter 4, aimed at evaluating the interest rate risk exposure of the thrifts it supervises.

## Chapter Four

# Measuring Interest Rate Risk

Of first concern to bankers in managing interest rate risk is measuring it. The projected effects of interest rate volatility on cash flows must be based on reliable measures of risk of interest rate changes along with measures of the value of assets, liabilities, and off–balance sheet elements. Once measurement is accomplished, workable risk management strategies can be selected and evaluated. In this chapter, we focus on the principal measurement techniques of interest rate risk. In the next chapter, we introduce and analyze various models of interest rate risk, including those of the federal bank regulatory agencies, that incorporate one or more of these measurement techniques with risk management strategies.

In measuring interest rate risk, two separate but complementary choices must be made. It is first necessary to choose a method for measuring the effects of changes in interest rates on values over the maturity and default risk spectrum—that is, the measurement methodology. Measurement methodologies include the now well-known techniques of "duration" and "asset-liability gap analysis," and the more recently developed "value at risk" (VaR).[1] It is then necessary to test the effects of such changes on the market value of the bank's portfolio or net worth—that is, the modeling methodology. Modeling methodologies include "worst-case scenario analysis," "stress tests" via simulated or assumed shocks (e.g., interest rates increase by 200 basis points), yield curve twist scenarios, Monte Carlo simulation, and an aspect of "value at risk" (VaR). Some approaches, like VaR, integrate measurement and modeling closely.

It is important to recognize that whatever methodologies are selected, there will be some common problems that must be resolved on an individual bank basis. One involves the response of bank depositors (and other bank creditors) to changes in market rates of interest. There has long been ample evidence that bank liabilities are sensitive to market rates. This has recently been revealed in the runoffs of bank CDs in the period from 1991 to the late fall of 1993 as market rates fell, and also in the difficulties banks had in raising new funds, without raising their own yields on deposits, as market rates rose in late 1993 throughout 1994. To some degree, however, the response will differ from bank to bank.

Another problem involves the extent to which individual transactions can be aggregated without forgoing an acceptable level of confidence in estimating interest rate risk exposure. The aggregation issue can be broken down into at least three elements: (1) a determination about aggregating individual balance sheet and off-balance sheet items into "maturity buckets," that is, determining the time classifications within which different items will be grouped; (2) a determination about groupings of items with the same market rate but differing repayment schedules, e.g., how installment loans with the same interest rate and maturity but with different repayment schedules are to be grouped; and (3) a determination about the level of detail of information required to support the computations decided on in (1) and (2).

In the next sections of this chapter, "duration" analysis, which lies at the core of the proposals now being offered by the federal banking agencies, is discussed. Alternative approaches, including an approach developed by the Office of Thrift Supervision (OTS), and VaR, such as J. P. Morgan's RiskMetrics, will then be reviewed. The chapter closes with a critique of these several measures.

## DURATION ANALYSIS

Duration analysis lies at the heart of most measures of interest rate risk and is commonly used as a tool in immunization and other risk control strategies. It is useful to briefly review its definition, computation, applicability to measurement, and limitations.

## The Price–Market Yield Relationship

At any given time, the relationship between the price, or market value, of a security of a certain maturity and a fixed cash flow is inversely related to the market yield-to-maturity (ytm) of instruments of like default risk, liquidity, and maturity.[2] Using the example of a 10-year default-free bond, a face value of $1,000, issued at par, and paying a 7 percent coupon interest semiannually, the price of this instrument at a 7 percent yield to maturity is $1,000. At a market yield to maturity of 9 percent, this bond will be priced at $869.92 (Table 4–1). The price of a fixed coupon bond is computed as follows:

$$P = \sum_{k=1}^{M} \frac{C}{(1 + \text{ytm}/f)^k} + \frac{F}{(1 + \text{ytm}/f)^M} \tag{1}$$

where $P$ is the market price of the bond, $C$ is the fixed coupon of one-half the annual coupon rate times the face value, $F$ is the face value of the bond ($1,000 in the example), $f$ is the payment frequency per year (2 in the example), ytm is the yield to maturity for the bond at this maturity, and $M$ is the number of periods to maturity (number of years times the frequency of payment). All payments are assumed to be made at the end of each period. Applying this formula to the bond with a ytm of 7 percent, $M$ of 20 periods (a 10-year maturity), $F$ of $1,000, $f$ of two payment periods per year, and a coupon payment of $35, the value of this bond is (Table 4–1):

$$P = \sum_{k=1}^{20} \frac{35}{(1 + 0.07/2)^k} + \frac{1,000}{(1 + 0.07/2)^{20}} = \$1,000 \tag{1a}$$

This bond is priced at par or $1,000.

Changes in market interest rates will affect the market values of securities such as the one in the example. Table 4–1 shows how the price of this security varies inversely with yields to maturity ranging from 0.5 percent to 22 percent. For example, if interest rates immediately rise, before the next coupon payment, to 9 percent—a 200 basis point (bp) rise—the value of the bond drops from $1,000 to $869.92, a decline of 13 percent in value for a 28 percent increase in interest rates. By contrast, a 200-bp decline in interest rates,

**TABLE 4-1**

| Yields, Bond Price, and Duration: 10-Year Maturity | | | | Yields, Bond Price, and Duration: 20-Year Maturity | | | |
|---|---|---|---|---|---|---|---|
| Yield | Price 10-yr | % ΔP | Duration 10-yr | Yield | Price 20-yr | % ΔP | Duration 20-yr |
| 0.005 | 1,633.25 |  | 8.00 | 0.005 | 2,235.65 |  | 14.10 |
| 0.010 | 1,569.62 | −3.90 | 7.95 | 0.010 | 2,085.17 | −6.73 | 13.88 |
| 0.015 | 1,508.97 | −3.86 | 7.91 | 0.015 | 1,947.29 | −6.61 | 13.66 |
| 0.020 | 1,451.14 | −3.83 | 7.86 | 0.020 | 1,820.87 | −6.49 | 13.43 |
| 0.025 | 1,395.98 | −3.80 | 7.81 | 0.025 | 1,704.86 | −6.37 | 13.20 |
| 0.030 | 1,343.37 | −3.77 | 7.76 | 0.030 | 1,598.32 | −6.25 | 12.97 |
| 0.035 | 1,293.18 | −3.74 | 7.72 | 0.035 | 1,500.40 | −6.13 | 12.73 |
| 0.040 | 1,245.27 | −3.70 | 7.67 | 0.040 | 1,410.33 | −6.00 | 12.49 |
| 0.045 | 1,199.55 | −3.67 | 7.62 | 0.045 | 1,327.42 | −5.88 | 12.26 |
| 0.050 | 1,155.89 | −3.64 | 7.56 | 0.050 | 1,251.03 | −5.75 | 12.02 |
| 0.055 | 1,114.20 | −3.61 | 7.51 | 0.055 | 1,180.59 | −5.63 | 11.77 |
| 0.060 | 1,074.39 | −3.57 | 7.46 | 0.060 | 1,115.57 | −5.51 | 11.53 |
| 0.065 | 1,036.35 | −3.54 | 7.41 | 0.065 | 1,055.52 | −5.38 | 11.29 |
| 0.070 | 1,000.00 | −3.51 | 7.35 | 0.070 | 1,000.00 | −5.26 | 11.05 |
| 0.075 | 965.26 | −3.47 | 7.30 | 0.075 | 948.62 | −5.14 | 10.81 |
| 0.080 | 932.05 | −3.44 | 7.25 | 0.080 | 901.04 | −5.02 | 10.57 |
| 0.085 | 900.29 | −3.41 | 7.19 | 0.085 | 856.92 | −4.90 | 10.34 |
| 0.090 | 869.92 | −3.37 | 7.14 | 0.090 | 815.98 | −4.78 | 10.10 |
| 0.095 | 840.87 | −3.34 | 7.08 | 0.095 | 777.96 | −4.66 | 9.87 |
| 0.100 | 813.07 | −3.31 | 7.02 | 0.100 | 742.61 | −4.54 | 9.64 |
| 0.105 | 786.46 | −3.27 | 6.97 | 0.105 | 709.72 | −4.43 | 9.41 |
| 0.110 | 760.99 | −3.24 | 6.91 | 0.110 | 679.08 | −4.32 | 9.19 |
| 0.115 | 736.61 | −3.20 | 6.85 | 0.115 | 650.51 | −4.21 | 8.97 |
| 0.120 | 713.25 | −3.17 | 6.79 | 0.120 | 623.84 | −4.10 | 8.76 |
| 0.125 | 690.88 | −3.14 | 6.73 | 0.125 | 598.93 | −3.99 | 8.54 |
| 0.130 | 669.44 | −3.10 | 6.68 | 0.130 | 575.63 | −3.89 | 8.34 |
| 0.135 | 648.90 | −3.07 | 6.62 | 0.135 | 553.83 | −3.79 | 8.14 |
| 0.140 | 629.21 | −3.03 | 6.56 | 0.140 | 533.39 | −3.69 | 7.94 |
| 0.145 | 610.33 | −3.00 | 6.50 | 0.145 | 514.22 | −3.59 | 7.75 |
| 0.150 | 592.22 | −2.97 | 6.44 | 0.150 | 496.22 | −3.50 | 7.56 |
| 0.155 | 574.85 | −2.93 | 6.38 | 0.155 | 479.31 | −3.41 | 7.37 |
| 0.160 | 558.18 | −2.90 | 6.32 | 0.160 | 463.39 | −3.32 | 7.20 |
| 0.165 | 542.19 | −2.87 | 6.26 | 0.165 | 448.40 | −3.23 | 7.02 |
| 0.170 | 526.83 | −2.83 | 6.20 | 0.170 | 434.27 | −3.15 | 6.86 |
| 0.175 | 512.09 | −2.80 | 6.14 | 0.175 | 420.94 | −3.07 | 6.69 |

**TABLE 4–1—*Continued***

| Yields, Bond Price, and Duration: 10-Year Maturity | | | | Yields, Bond Price, and Duration: 20-Year Maturity | | | |
|---|---|---|---|---|---|---|---|
| Yield | Price 10-yr | % ΔP | Duration 10-yr | Yield | Price 20-yr | % ΔP | Duration 20-yr |
| 0.180 | 497.93 | –2.77 | 6.08 | 0.180 | 408.35 | –2.99 | 6.54 |
| 0.185 | 484.33 | –2.73 | 6.01 | 0.185 | 396.44 | –2.92 | 6.38 |
| 0.190 | 471.26 | –2.70 | 5.95 | 0.190 | 385.17 | –2.84 | 6.24 |
| 0.195 | 458.69 | –2.67 | 5.89 | 0.195 | 374.49 | –2.77 | 6.09 |
| 0.200 | 446.62 | –2.63 | 5.83 | 0.200 | 364.36 | –2.70 | 5.95 |
| 0.205 | 435.01 | –2.60 | 5.77 | 0.205 | 354.75 | –2.64 | 5.82 |
| 0.210 | 423.84 | –2.57 | 5.71 | 0.210 | 345.62 | –2.57 | 5.69 |
| 0.215 | 413.09 | –2.54 | 5.65 | 0.215 | 336.94 | –2.51 | 5.57 |
| 0.220 | 402.75 | –2.50 | 5.59 | 0.220 | 328.67 | –2.45 | 5.45 |

from 7 percent to 5 percent, results in a bond value of $1,155.89 and a 16 percent increase in value for a 28 percent decrease in interest rates.

## Definition of Duration

The relationship between bond prices and market interest rates can be measured in a number of ways. For example, the increase in interest rates of 200 bp when the yield to maturity is 7 percent leads to a price decrease of $130.08, or by 13 percent. In contrast, consider the effect of the same 200-bp increase in interest rates if market yield levels are at 12 percent. In this case, the price of the security falls to $629.21 from $713.25, by $84.04 and 12 percent (see Table 4–1). In short, the price effect of a given change in market yields depends on the level of yields and, as we will see later, the shape of the yield curve.

Another factor that affects the relationship between market interest rate changes and a security's price is its remaining maturity. Barring any irregularities in the cash flow from a security, a coupon bond of the same yield, coupon, and face value will have greater interest rate sensitivity the longer its maturity. The results of interest rate changes on the value of bonds of different maturities are shown in Table 4–1 and Figure 4–1. The two securities are the 10-year 7 percent security in the above examples and a 20-year-maturity security with a 7 percent coupon payable semiannually, a face value of $1,000, and selling at par at a yield to maturity of 7 percent. If we consider the interest rate increase of 200 bp at a market yield to maturity from both bonds of 7 percent, the security with the 20-year maturity has a price decline of $182.04, whereas the 10-year-maturity security exhibits only a $130.08 decline. Although in the markets, yields on 20-year bonds may not fluctuate by the same amount as yields on 10-year bonds, the potential price volatility is greater for the longer-maturity instrument. Consequently, measures of price sensitivity of securities to market interest rate changes should incorporate the maturity of the security.

One measure that attempts to incorporate the yield level, maturity, timing of cash flows, and change in market interest rates, abstracting from the amount of the change in interest rates, is the measure of duration. This relationship was first described by Macaulay (1938) in applications regarding insurance investments. Duration is a measure of the price sensitivity of an instrument to interest rate changes and is defined as the proportional change in the price of an instrument resulting from the proportional change in the yield to maturity factor, $(1 + \text{ytm}/f)$. The interpretation that is made of duration as defined is as the elasticity of price of a security from a change in market interest rates. It should also be emphasized that the interest rate change takes place over the entire spectrum of maturities such that securities of all maturities experience the same increase in yields to maturity.

Macaulay's duration can also be thought of in terms of the time-weighted average of cash flows over the maturity of the instrument. Designating Macaulay's duration as $D_M$, this interpretation is computed as follows:

$$D_M = \frac{\displaystyle\sum_{k=1}^{M} \frac{kC}{(1 + \text{ytm}/f)^k} + \frac{MF}{(1 + \text{ytm}/f)^M}}{P} \tag{2}$$

The units of measure of $D_M$ are in terms of time and in the time interval units of the yield to maturity, years in the case of our examples.[3] For example, the 10-year bond in Table 4–1 has a duration of

**FIGURE 4–1**
*Price–Interest Rate Relationship (10-Yr and 20-Yr bonds, 7% Coupon)*

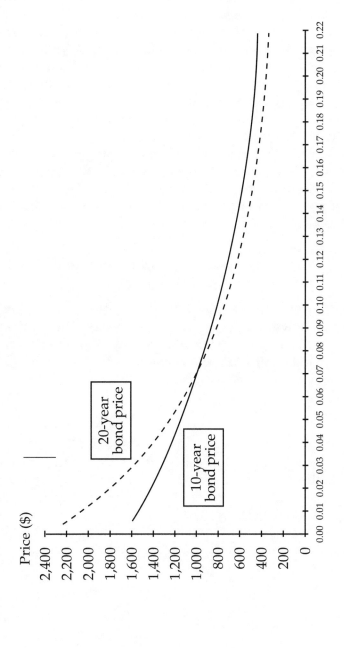

7.35 years when the yield to maturity is 7 percent; the 20-year bond with the same yield has a duration of 11.05 years. The sign of the duration measure is negative because of the inverse relationship between market interest rates and price of the instrument. The longer the maturity of an instrument, all other factors the same, the greater (more negative) the value of Macaulay's duration. This can be seen in Figure 4–2, which plots the duration of the 10-year and 20-year maturity bonds in our examples (see Table 4–1) as positive values. Duration of the 20-year bond is considerably higher than that of the 10-year bond at low levels of interest rates. But just as the percentage price change of a bond will decline at higher yields in response to a given change in interest rates, both durations decline as interest rates rise, with the duration of the 10-year bond and the 20-year bond about the same at a yield to maturity of 21 percent.

### Measuring Market Price Changes Using Duration and Problems of Convexity

From the definition of duration as the elasticity of a change in an asset's price with respect to a change in yield to maturity, the market price change can be estimated for a given proportional change in the yield to maturity factor. Defining Macaulay's duration algebraically in terms of an elasticity:

$$D_M \equiv \frac{\partial P}{\partial \text{ytm}} \frac{(1 + \text{ytm})}{P} \qquad (3)$$

where the $\partial P / \partial \text{ytm}$ is the partial derivative of the price with respect to the interest rate change. We use the partial here in order to make it clear that there are other factors that can lead to price changes that are held constant.

Rewriting equation (3) gives the proportional price change in terms of the level of duration and the proportional change in the interest factor:

$$\frac{\partial P}{P} = D_M \frac{\partial \text{ytm}}{(1 + \text{ytm}/f)} \qquad (4)$$

**FIGURE 4–2**
*Interest Rate–Duration Relationship*

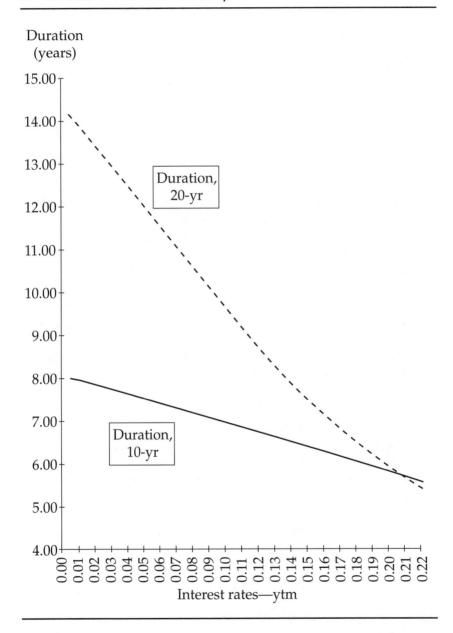

The sign of this relationship depends on the direction of change in ytm—if interest rates rise, the sign is negative because the sign of duration is negative.

In putting values to this formula, it should be noted that this relationship is developed for small changes in interest rates. Applying this to the bond data in Table 4–1 and using the 7 percent ytm, 10-year bond at the par value of $1,000 and considering a change in rates of 0.5 percent (50 bp), the value of the actual proportional price change is –3.51 percent (Table 4–1). Using equation (4), the resulting calculation is:

$$\frac{\partial P}{P} = (-7.35)\frac{0.005}{(1.035)} = -3.56\%$$

The difference between the actual change and the duration-based estimate is due to the incomplete nature of the estimate. It does not take into account that the price-yield relationship is not linear, but is bowed or convex for normal securities. This convexity is clearly evident in Figure 4–1, showing that the 20-year bond has a greater bow and is, thus, more convex than the 10-year bond. Therefore, any change in yield must account for movement at the point of change *and* the convex shape of the price-yield relationship. Duration accounts for the price movement due to an interest rate change at the initial price of the bond, but it does not take into consideration the nonlinear nature of the change in price as interest rates change.

The convexity of a relationship can be measured by taking the total proportional change in the price, rather than a partial change, in response to an interest rate change. This is accomplished by approximating the total change using a mathematical technique of a Taylor expansion that takes into consideration higher-order changes.

The proportional change in price due to an interest rate change is a duration term plus a convexity term. This is:

$$\frac{dP}{P} = D_M\frac{dytm}{(1 + ytm)} + \frac{1}{2}\frac{\partial^2 P}{\partial ytm^2}\frac{1}{P}dytm^2 \tag{5}$$

(See the Appendix to this chapter for the derivation of this relationship.)

The second term in this relationship measures convexity times the square of the change in the yield to maturity. The convexity term is commonly expressed as:

$$\text{Convexity} = \frac{1}{2} \frac{\partial^2 P}{\partial \text{ytm}^2} \frac{1}{P} d\text{ytm}^2 \tag{6}$$

The sign of this term is positive for normal securities such as Treasury bonds without a call feature, since the change in the price due to an interest rate change, taking into account only duration, is always a smaller increase or a larger decrease in price than would be the actual change. Thus, price increases, due to interest rate declines, need to be increased; and price decreases, due to interest rate increases, are overstated and need to be decreased (made less negative).

The example of an overstated price decline due to an interest rate increase of 50 bp is shown in the –3.56 percent estimate above. The measure of convexity developed in equation (6) calculates the total adjustment due to convexity (including the squared interest rate change) in the above example as 0.04 percent. Thus, adjusting the –3.56 percent estimate of the percentage price change by 0.04 gives a convexity-adjusted proportional price change of –3.52 percent. This is considerably closer to the actual, calculated percentage change in price for a 50-bp increase in rates of –3.51 percent. The greater the change in interest rates, the greater the relative importance of the convexity adjustment relative to the actual percentage change in price.

Larger changes, such as 200-bp changes, are more difficult to approximate simply with duration. For example, starting with a duration of –7.35 years at an interest rate of 7 percent for the 10-year security, a 200-bp increase in interest rates will lower the security's value to $869.92 (Table 4–1). This represents a 13.01 percent actual decline in the price. In contrast, the duration formula, unadjusted for convexity [equation (4)], estimates the decline as:

$$\frac{dP}{P} = D_M \frac{0.02}{1.035} = -7.35 \frac{0.02}{1.035} = -14.24\%$$

The overstatement is 123 bp. The convexity correction in equation (6) provides an adjustment of 64 bp. The adjusted estimate, based on duration, is then 13.6 percent, closer to the actual proportional price change of 13.01 percent, but hardly perfect. This imprecision is traceable to the assumed large change in interest rates. In the example, a 200-bp rise in interest rates from 7.0 percent to 9.0 percent causes the slope of the price–interest rate relationship to become less negative and duration to change accordingly from –7.35 years to –7.14 years (Table 4–1). However, when using the duration formula to estimate changes in bond values, the value of duration is assumed to be constant and the convexity correction is only a partial correction for the change in slope. Thus, for large changes in interest rates, duration with convexity adjustments remains only an approximation.

## *The Problem of Negative Convexity— Embedded Options*

Debt instruments that we have so far discussed have had cash flows that are independent of market interest rates or free of some degree of optionality. There are many types of instruments that have embedded options, including corporate and government bonds with call features and mortgage and mortgage-backed securities (MBS) with prepayment features. Of particular importance to bankers is the option depositors have to withdraw deposits (or place deposits) and close accounts at will, although subject to some withdrawal penalties.

A common example of embedded options facing banks arises in the prepayment option on home mortgages—that is, the right, but not the obligation, of the borrower to call back the loan from the mortgage lender. The effect of the prepayment option is to reduce the value of the mortgage or MBS (GNMA, FNMA, Freddie Mac, or private MBS) with no prepayment option by an estimate of the discounted expected value of the loss from the prepayment. Although mortgage prepayment can arise for many reasons, the volume is inversely related to the level of interest rates—the lower are interest rates, the more likely prepayment will occur because of refinancing on existing mortgages or repayment due to interest rate incentives to change residences.

As a result of the embedded option, the price–interest rate relationship is no longer convex, but may be bowed in the opposite direction; that is, it may become concave to the origin of the graph of price or value and interest rates, or exhibit negative convexity.

**FIGURE 4–3**
*Convexity in the Price–Interest Rate Relationship*

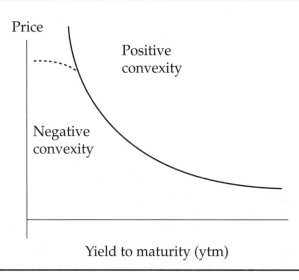

Figure 4–3 provides a graphical view of an investment, from the investor's perspective, that has a negative convexity portion at low rates of interest. The slope of the price–interest rate relationship is negative, giving rise to a negative duration. But in the upper portion (at low interest rates), the curve "bows" away from the origin (dotted line in Figure 4–3); that is, the upper portion of the curve, while still having a negative slope, is negatively convex.[4]

The value of a debt instrument with embedded options can be considered to be the value of the identical instrument without an embedded option, less the value of the option. If the level of interest rates were the only factor determining option value, then the value of the option is the value of a call option on an interest rate contract that mimicked the repayment behavior of mortgagors (at different maturities over the life of their mortgages)—or, alternatively, the MBS with the investor viewed as the option writer. This approach can be represented as follows:

Price of MBS (with prepayment option) = Price of MBS
(without prepayment) – Call option                             (7)

The holders of such assets incur a reinvestment risk. Their potential loss is the difference between the present value of the cash flows if the mortgage were held to maturity less the present value of the cash flows that can be earned on the repaid principal at the current rate of interest on equivalent default-free investments.[5] Consequently, if current interest rates are lower than the contract rate on the mortgage being repaid, the mortgage investor cannot reinvest the repayment at the same return and will take a loss. On the other hand, if interest rates are higher than the contract rate, the mortgage investor actually can gain by any repayment. But a significant volume of repayments are more likely to be associated with lower interest rates.[6]

Negative convexity is a risk that the banker must absorb when investing in such instruments. It can be measured and adjusted for when considering the interest rate risk profile of different investments subject to embedded options. These adjustments have been accounted for in the agencies' proposal to some degree and more consistently in the OTS model. Others, such as the "value at risk" proposal of the Basle Committee, skirt the problem by ignoring such investment instruments entirely.

### Twists of the Yield Curve and Alternative Measures of Duration and Adjustments for Single Instruments

The assumption concerning changes in interest rates in interpreting the meaning of duration as a measure of interest rate sensitivity of an instrument has been that changes are equal at each maturity. This means that the yield curve will shift upward or downward in a parallel manner (by the same amount) from its initial position. This assumption serves to emphasize the static nature of duration measures and represents a severe limitation in its use as a general measure of interest rate sensitivity. Analytical measures of interest rate risk exposure based on duration and allowing for term structure twists and nonparallel changes require models of the generation of the yield curve. These models have proliferated over the past 15 years and represent a cottage industry. However, there is no model that has proven best. This will be discussed more thoroughly in Chapter 5 when we cover the modeling of interest rate changes in any of the overall frameworks for assessing interest rate risk.

## PORTFOLIO RELATIONSHIPS AND DURATION MEASURES

The potential impact on a portfolio of interest rate changes is commonly evaluated through the analysis of duration by calculating the time-weighted present values of the cash flows emanating from financial instruments making up the portfolio. Duration analysis underlies the earlier proposal by the banking agencies for incorporating interest rate risk into risk-adjusted capital requirements (Federal Reserve Board, September 14, 1993). As implied by the discussion of the duration of a single instrument, the duration of a portfolio can also measure the elasticity of a portfolio's market value with respect to changes in market yields.[7]

The duration of a portfolio is defined as the weighted sum of the duration of the assets and liabilities of the portfolio. The weights are the share of the assets of the portfolio. The agencies' proposal is in terms of the proportional change in the economic value of assets and liabilities due to a hypothesized change in interest rates.[8] These proportional changes in assets and liabilities of a bank can be accumulated to provide a calculation for the change in the economic value of a bank's capital relative to its assets, thus arriving at a measure of the sensitivity of equity to changes in interest rates. A simple model is helpful.[9]

The balance sheet accounting identity (using market values of assets and liabilities) is:

$$A \equiv L + E \tag{8}$$

where $A$ is bank total assets, $L$ is liabilities, and $E$ is equity. The change in a bank's asset market value is then defined as:

$$dA \equiv dL + dE \tag{9}$$

In terms of a proportional change in each of the components expressed in terms of their share of assets:

$$\frac{dA}{A} \equiv \frac{dL}{L}\frac{L}{A} + \frac{dE}{E}\frac{E}{A} \tag{9a}$$

Rewriting this relationship in terms of the proportional change in equity gives:

$$\frac{dE}{E} \equiv \left(\frac{dA}{A} - \frac{dL}{L}\frac{L}{A}\right)\frac{A}{E} \tag{9b}$$

As we show in more detail in the chapter Appendix, using a Taylor expansion of the change in $A$ and $L$ about a given yield to maturity, $y_A$ and $y_L$, and ignoring all polynomial terms after the powers of 2, the proportional change in assets and liabilities [as in equation (5) above] can be stated as:

$$\frac{dA}{A} = \left[\frac{\partial A}{\partial y_A}dy_A + \frac{1}{2}\frac{\partial^2 A}{\partial y_A^2}dy_A^2\right]\bigg/ A$$

$$\tag{10}$$

$$\frac{dL}{L} = \left[\frac{\partial L}{\partial y_L}dy_L + \frac{1}{2}\frac{\partial^2 L}{\partial y_L^2}dy_L^2\right]\bigg/ L$$

The sign of the first partial derivative is almost always negative, arising from a negative price-yield relationship. The second partial derivative normally has a positive sign, indicating that the slope of the price-yield relationship gets flatter (less negative) as market yields rise (the exception to a negative value is for instruments at interest rates where there is an embedded option). For small interest rate changes, the second partial derivative is near zero, but for larger changes this "convexity" component of the price-yield relationship is important for properly evaluating the full changes in value due to interest rate changes. The total effect normally will carry a negative sign (see examples in the previous section and Table 4–1).

Each of these equations can be rewritten in terms of measures of duration using the elasticity definition for Macaulay's duration for assets, $D_A$, and liabilities, $D_L$:

$$D_A \equiv \frac{\partial A}{\partial y_A}\frac{(1+y_A)}{A} \qquad D_L \equiv \frac{\partial L}{\partial y_L}\frac{(1+y_L)}{L} \tag{11}$$

Equation (10) can be expressed in terms of duration accounting for the convexity factor adjustment as follows:

$$\frac{dA}{A} = \frac{\partial A}{\partial y_A} \frac{(1 + y_A)}{A} \frac{dy_A}{(1 + y_A)} + \frac{1}{2} \frac{\partial^2 A}{\partial y_A^2} \frac{dy_A^2}{A}$$

$$\frac{dL}{L} = \frac{\partial L}{\partial y_L} \frac{(1 + y_L)}{L} \frac{dy_L}{(1 + y_L)} + \frac{1}{2} \frac{\partial^2 L}{\partial y_L^2} \frac{dy_L^2}{L}$$

(12)

Equations (12) can be rewritten in terms of duration and convexity [see equation (6) above] as:

$$\frac{dA}{A} = D_A \frac{dy_A}{(1 + y_A)} + \frac{1}{2} \frac{\partial^2 A}{\partial y_A^2} \frac{dy_A^2}{A}$$

$$\frac{dL}{L} = D_L \frac{dy_L}{(1 + y_L)} + \frac{1}{2} \frac{\partial^2 L}{\partial y_L^2} \frac{dy_L^2}{L}$$

(12a)

Substituting equations (12a) into equation (9b) gives the proportional change in the value of bank equity (a bank portfolio) in terms of the weighted difference in durations times the interest rate changes for assets and liabilities and the weighted convexities:

$$\frac{dE}{E} = \left( D_A \frac{dy_A}{(1 + y_A)} + \frac{1}{2} \frac{\partial^2 A}{\partial y_A^2} \frac{dy_A^2}{A} - D_L \frac{dy_L}{(1 + y_L)} \frac{L}{A} - \frac{1}{2} \frac{\partial^2 L}{\partial y_L^2} \frac{dy_L^2}{L} \frac{L}{A} \right) \frac{A}{E}$$

(13)

The term $D_A/(1 + y_A)$ is known as "modified duration" of assets, and $D_L/(1 + y_L)$ is the modified duration for liabilities. These are assumed to remain unchanged for interest rate changes, since the interest rates referred to, $y_A$ and $y_L$, in this case, are the initial interest rates from which any change is taken. From this relationship, and being consistent with the use of duration measures for analysis of interest sensitivity by assuming $dy_A$ and $dy_L$ are equal (a parallel yield curve shift), it is clear that if the market value of a bank's equity is to be immune from interest rate changes, the term in brackets in equation (13) must be zero.[10] Thus, the bank would need to have matched not only the modified duration of assets and the weighted modified duration of liabilities, but the convexities of assets and weighted liabilities as well. The weight in these cases is the ratio of the market value of liabilities to the market value of assets $(L/A)$.[11] In this regard, it is also interesting to note that as the leverage of the bank increases $(A/E$ increases and $L/A$ increases), the proportional change in equity becomes more negative. Thus, greater leverage increases the interest rate sensitivity of the market value of equity.

## Twists of the Yield Curve and Other Interest Rate Assumptions of a Portfolio

The assumption of a parallel shift of the yield curve—that is, equal changes in yields at each maturity and for each type of asset and liability—in arriving at results on the sensitivity of individual instruments, portfolios, and equity to interest rate changes is fairly common and had been adopted in the earlier banking agencies' proposal. In interpreting the meaning of duration as a measure of interest rate sensitivity of an instrument, the assumption has been that changes are equal at each maturity. The assumption makes duration analysis "static," and constitutes a severe limitation in its use as a general measure of interest rate sensitivity for portfolios in particular. Measures of interest rate risk exposure based on duration and allowing for term structure twists—that is, nonparallel changes—require additional models of the generation of the yield curve. In addition, the assumption that interest rate changes are the same for each type of instrument, regardless of default risk characteristics, over their entire maturity may be a greater limitation on duration analysis as a general measure of interest rate sensitivity. At present, however, there is no model that has been proven best, or even adequate to address the term structure issue or the default risk issue. These problems will be discussed more thoroughly in Chapter 5 when we cover the modeling of interest rate changes in the overall frameworks for assessing interest rate risk.

## THE VALUE-AT-RISK (VaR) MEASURE OF INTEREST RATE RISK

There have been a number of proposals that have suggested the use of a concept known as value at risk (VaR) to evaluate so-called market risks, a class of risk inclusive of interest rate risk. Market risk includes the risk of losses on debt instruments, equities, foreign exchange, and commodities arising from movements in any of their market prices. The proposals most important for banks and other depository institutions are those made by the Basle Committee on Bank Supervision to amend the 1988 agreement, released in May 1995. The proposal itself applies to large, international banks and specifically to their trading activities. It explicitly excludes "interest rate risk for the whole bank." Nevertheless, it recommends using VaR to measure market risk due to interest rates, among other market factors. The specifics of the proposal are discussed more fully in Chapter 5.

In reviewing the components of VaR in this chapter, we draw on the Basle Proposal (1995), J. P. Morgan's public implementation of VaR known as *RiskMetrics,* and a proposal by Green and Mark (1994) for an implementation at Manufacturers Hanover Trust. Each of these proposes a different modeling approach, but the implementation and problems of VaR as a measure of interest rate risk are practically the same.

The term "value at risk" (VaR) has become synonymous with sophisticated measurement and modeling of the effects of changes in market conditions on possible losses from portfolios in trading accounts, proprietary trading positions, and derivatives positions. As noted above, VaR is defined as the maximum estimated loss in market value, at a specified probability, of a given position over a horizon sufficiently long such that the position can be neutralized or liquidated. In the discussion, we will present VaR as an index to measure interest rate risk in the same way that duration is an index that measures similar risk. In fact, it will become clear that

VaR and duration are closely related measures of interest rate risk because duration forms the basis for the measure of interest rate sensitivity of a position in the VaR implementations.

Finally we will show that duration and VaR are static measures in the sense that they are the first-order change in market value of an investment or a position with respect to a change in interest rates (more generally, market conditions).[12] In short, both are measures of delta risk—changes in market value due to changes in interest rates. The volatility of interest rate changes on market values (vega risk) is ignored in duration and VaR, while convexity adjustments account for "gamma" risk in both approaches.

The significance of interest rate volatility is that greater volatility creates greater price or value variations for a portfolio. Of particular concern for banks is that greater interest rate volatility gives rise to a greater chance that losses will arise due strictly to interest rate changes and that interest rate term structure predictability is impaired. In practice, measures of price volatility of interest-bearing securities are measures of the standard deviation of proportional changes in price and are derived from measures of interest rate volatility through the use of duration values for zero-coupon securities. Specifically, the volatility of security prices is the product of the volatility of yield changes times the measure of modified duration times the yield.[13] Algebraically, this is:

$$\text{Volatility}_{\text{price}} = (\text{Volatility}_{\text{yield}}) \, \frac{D_M}{(1 + Yield)} \, (\text{Yield}) \tag{14}$$

We will use this relationship when computing price volatility and substitute estimates of the standard deviation of proportional interest rate changes as proxies for yield volatility.

The use of VaR requires the selection of several more or less arbitrary values. The first involves the length of the horizon, or the period over which a position can be liquidated, reversed, or otherwise neutralized. The actual horizon used depends upon the liquidity of the position and its components, since more liquid positions can be neutralized more rapidly. Thus, within a portfolio, there may be positions that differ in their ability to be liquidated, reversed, or neutralized.

The second choice involves the stochastic behavior of market-related variables. In most implementations, the stochastic properties assumed include a joint normal distribution of returns on positions, no correlation between returns of different periods, and a stable process over time.[14] This process is usually referred to as a stable random walk, with relative prices defined as either discrete proportional changes, $(P_t - P_{t-1})/P_{t-1}$, or as the natural logarithm of the ratio of current to last period's price, $\ln(P_t/P_{t-1})$. For short time periods and reasonably small price changes, the computed values are very nearly equal. The logarithmic difference is consistent with continuous-time approaches to valuing financial contracts.[15]

### Value at Risk for a Position Composed of a Single Security or Instrument

Focusing on interest rate changes, the VaR value for a position in a single security, $i$, is defined as:

$$\text{VaR}_i \equiv V_i \frac{dV_i}{dP_i} \Delta P_i \tag{15}$$

where $\text{VaR}_i$ is the value at risk measure for the position, $V_i$ is the current market value of the position, $dV_i/dP_i$ is the sensitivity to a price move in the security per dollar of market value, and $\Delta P_i$ is the specified price move per horizon period. Measurement of VaR for a security requires estimation of the values for sensitivity and the change in price. The approach used in most applications of measuring value at risk of a security due to interest rate risk is to note that the position value, $V_i$, will change by \$1 for every \$1 change in price and to approximate $\Delta P_i$ by a duration-based measure. Rewriting equation (4) in terms of a proportional change in a security's price:

$$\frac{dP_i}{P_i} = \frac{D_M}{(1 + y_i)} dy_i \tag{16}$$

where $D_M$ is Macaulay's duration, discussed above, of the security measured at the current interest rate, $y_i$, $P_i$ is the current market value of a single security evaluated using $y_i$; and $dy_i$ is the hypothesized change in interest rate.[16]

The choice of the change in interest rate is determined by the choice of confidence level and horizon period. For example, if a one-day horizon is chosen for this particular position, the hypothesized change in interest rate would be based on the distribution of one-day interest rate changes. If the chosen horizon is one month, then distribution of one-month changes is used. The specified confidence level requires the selection of horizon, since it is the horizon which specifies the probability distribution that is to be used—namely, the values of mean and standard deviation of interest rate change. The value of $dy_i$ that is hypothesized is defined, then, as the change in interest rate at an $\alpha$ confidence level over a specified horizon:

$$dy_i \equiv y_i (\mu_{dy} + k_\alpha \sigma_{dy}) \tag{17}$$

where $\mu_{dy}$ is the mean estimated proportional change in the interest rate, $k_\alpha$ is the multiple of standard deviations from the mean corresponding to an $\alpha$ confidence level, and $\sigma_{dy}$ is the estimated standard deviation. For example, at a 90 percent confidence level (two-tailed), $k_\alpha$ is 1.65.

For interest rate value-at-risk analysis, the measure of $VaR_i$ is operationally defined for computational purposes as [substituting equations (16) and (17) into equation (15)]:

$$VaR_i \equiv V_i \frac{D_M}{(1 + y_i)} y_i(\mu_{dy} + k_\alpha \sigma_{dy}) \tag{18}$$

Note that this relationship essentially estimates the volatility of prices, $\Delta P_i$, using equation (14). An example using this relationship is for a 10-year zero-coupon bond denominated in French francs (FFR) for a position of FFR100 million at maturity.[17] The duration of this bond is 10 years, the current interest rate on the bond is 7.96 percent, and the bond is priced at FFR46.5 per FFR100 par. For the position in this security, a daily horizon is chosen for measuring VaR. The value of the position, $V_i$, is FFR46.5 million, the mean daily interest rate change is 0.192 percent, and the daily standard deviation of interest rate changes is 1.181 percent. Using equation (18) for these values and a 90 percent confidence level gives:

$$VaR_i \equiv (46.5) \frac{10}{(1.0796)} (0.0796)[0.00192 + (1.65)(0.01181)]$$

$$= FFR0.733920 \; million = FFR733,920$$

This magnitude implies that 1.6 percent of the value of the position is at risk from daily interest rate changes. Another way of interpreting this risk is to consider the risk of loss in terms of days. Thus, a 5 percent probability of this loss or greater occurring daily means that this loss or greater is likely to occur in 1 day out of 20 (1/0.05 days). If the position can be liquidated within a single day, as projected by the choice of a daily horizon, and is managed efficiently, the 20-day likely event window is long (nearly a 1-month trading period) and may well exceed the planned holding period of the position.

### Value at Risk for a Portfolio Composed of Positions of Securities or Instruments

The value at risk for a portfolio that may be composed of long and short positions in interest rate contracts is directly related to standard portfolio analysis. Using a two-position portfolio to develop the VaR for a portfolio, the value of the portfolio at time $t$ is the sum of the market values of the two positions:[18]

$$V_p \equiv V_1 + V_2 \tag{19}$$

The return on the portfolio can be defined as the proportional rate of change of the value of the portfolio, $dV_p/V_p$, and is the weighted sum of the returns on each position:

$$\frac{dV_p}{V_p} \equiv w_1 \frac{dV_1}{V_1} + w_2 \frac{dV_2}{V_2} \tag{20}$$

where $w_1 + w_2 = 1$. The variance of the return on the portfolio, $\sigma_p^2$, is found by taking the variance of $dV_p/V_p$ and is defined as:

$$\sigma_p^2 \equiv w_1^2 \sigma_1^2 + w_2^2 \sigma_2^2 + 2w_1 w_2 \, \text{cov}(R_1, R_2) \tag{21}$$

where $\text{cov}(R_1, R_2)$ is the covariance of the returns of each position and $R_i$ is shorthand for $dV_i/V_i$.

Following the definition of value at risk given in equation (15), the VaR for a portfolio is defined in the same way as:

$$\text{VaR}_p \equiv V_p \frac{dV_p}{dV_p} \Delta V_p \tag{22}$$

Noting that the sensitivity term, $dV_p/dV_p$, is 1 and the $\Delta V_p$ is the $k_\alpha$ standard deviation of the portfolio value change, $\text{VaR}_p$ can be rewritten as:

$$\text{VaR}_p \equiv V_p k_\alpha \sigma_p \tag{23}$$

Using equation (21), noting that $w_i$ is $V_i/V_p$, and squaring both sides of equation (23):

$$\text{VaR}_p^2 = V_p^2 k_a^2 \big[ w_1^2 \sigma_1^2 + w_2^2 \sigma_2^2 + 2w_1 w_2 \, cov(R_1, R_2) \big]^2 \tag{24}$$

Collecting terms, noting that $w_i V_p$ is $V_i$, and expressing the covariance of the returns in terms of the correlation between the returns:

$$\text{VaR}_p \equiv \big[ V_1^2 \, k_a^2 \, \sigma_1^2 + V_2^2 \, k_\alpha^2 \sigma_2^2 + 2V_1 V_2 \rho_{1,2} \sigma_1 \sigma_2 \big]^{1/2} \tag{25}$$

By definition of VaR for a single portfolio, the value at risk for a portfolio is then:

$$\text{VaR}_p \equiv \big[ \text{VaR}_1^2 + \text{VaR}_2^2 + 2\text{VaR}_1 \text{VaR}_2 \, \rho_{1,2} \big]^{1/2} \tag{26}$$

From this expression, a portfolio value at risk incorporates the correlation of the changes in the returns among the component positions in the portfolio and the individual position VaRs.[19]

As discussed above, calculations of $\text{VaR}_p$ for interest rate risk assessment purposes utilize duration measures to evaluate each of the $\text{VaR}_i$ for component positions. Accordingly, the correlation coefficient, $\rho_{1,2}$, must be measured as the correlation between the market yield proportional changes on the different securities corresponding to the specified position restructuring horizon period. This approach assumes that the interest rate movements over the specified horizon are sufficiently small that duration for each component position can be taken as a constant. If this were not the case, then the correlation of price changes derived from interest rate changes would need to incorporate changes in duration due to changes in interest. To a considerable extent, this assumption is met, since the duration measures are applied to zero-coupon bond equivalent interest rates with constant maturity; in these cases, duration is equal to the length of the maturity.

## Interpreting Portfolio VaR

Portfolio VaR incorporates historical interest rate volatility and cor-relations among interest rate changes into a measure of interest rate risk. Using historical data along with equation (26), portfolio VaR can be readily computed from the VaRs of the separate portfolio po-sitions, whether they be long positions in single securities, short po-sitions, or off–balance sheet derivative positions. From the stand-point of risk assessment, the portfolio VaR measure is superior to simply adding the VaRs of each position, since gains for risk man-agement can be achieved from diversification effects among posi-tions. This means that a bank can offset its risks in one type of posi-tion, say, an asset, with a short position in an instrument that will offer an inverse correlation with the returns on the long position.

An example of the portfolio relationship is to refer back to the structure of the bank as a set of assets and liabilities and the mar-ket value of the bank as the difference between the market values of assets and liabilities—equations (9), (9a), and (9b). The value at risk for the bank as a portfolio due to interest rate changes can be defined as follows:[20]

$$VaR_E \equiv \left[VaR_A^2 + VaR_L^2 + 2VaR_A VaR_L \rho_{A,L}\right]^{1/2} \tag{27}$$

The sign of the last term in this relationship is negative because of the definition of the proportional change in equity as the propor-tional change in assets' market value minus the proportional change in liabilities' market value as in equation (9a). This means that although there is a positive correlation for interest rate changes between assets and liabilities, as there is likely to be, the VaR for the entire bank portfolio (excluding off–balance sheet items for now) is reduced compared with the simple addition of the VaRs for the two components of the portfolio.

The implication of the portfolio VaR can be emphasized using an example with extreme values. Consider the case where the VaRs for assets and liabilities are of equal magnitudes and interest rate changes are perfectly correlated between them. The portfolio VaR in this case is zero. Putting the VaRs in terms of VaR for assets:

$$VaR_E \equiv \left[2VaR_A^2 - 2VaR_A^2\right]^{1/2} \tag{28}$$

This simply means that if assets and liabilities have the same interest sensitivity characteristics, the effects of interest rate changes and volatility on bank market value of equity will be neutralized in this type of portfolio—the bank will not have interest rate risk. It also demonstrates the importance of including the correlations among asset and liability interest rate changes in measuring portfolio VaR.

## OFFICE OF THRIFT SUPERVISION MEASURES

Inasmuch as OTS measures of interest rate risk are duration-based, they suffer from the same deficiencies as the pure duration-based measures employed by the banking agencies. However, the OTS measurement is an improvement in several respects. In particular, it tries to measure optionality on mortgage-backed securities and attempts to value interest rate options such as interest rate caps and floors. The drawback to the OTS measurement is that it is strictly a delta measure of value changes with regard to interest rates and ignores volatility and its variation. Although the OTS methods are more detailed than the banking agencies' 1993 proposal, they suffer from most of the same limitations. A more complete analysis of the modeling used by OTS will be presented in Chapter 5.

## A CRITIQUE OF THE MEASURES
## AND CONCLUSIONS

Duration is an approximation to interest rate sensitivity of financial instruments and portfolios. It becomes a worse approximation the more convex is a financial instrument and when the instrument exhibits negative convexity. Highly convex instruments are characterized by longer term and higher coupon (see Figure 4–1). Shorter-term instruments are less convex, while zero-coupon instruments, with no optionality, exhibit a constant duration over all interest rate states. Although duration is widely used as a tool for interest rate risk hedging, it is only a second-order approximation, even after accounting for convexity. Large changes in interest rates cause a wide disparity between actual and duration-based estimates of changes in market value. From a risk assessment perspective, the duration-based measure is conservative, since it overstates the decline in value with an increase in interest rates for most instruments. However, when interest rates decline, duration-based estimates will considerably overstate the increase in market value for instruments or portfolios with meaningful optionality. Therefore, the presence of optionality is a serious challenge to the use of duration-based measures as proxies for measures of interest rate sensitivity and interest rate risk.

Another drawback to duration-based measures is that they ignore risks due to changes in interest rate volatility. By its definition, duration only measures changes in value due to changes in interest rates. Greater interest rate volatility is not accounted for by duration, and using duration-based measures for hedging purposes limits the hedge to delta interest rate hedging. Increases in interest rate volatility amount to increases in risk, since larger interest rate changes are possible with the same likelihood. Consequently, this source of risk can only be handled using duration-based measures by imposing larger interest rate changes when performing risk evaluation.

This measurement is incomplete, since interest rate volatility is itself not predictable and is subject to serious variation. These sources of risk are prominent causes of twists in the yield curve. When interest rate changes have low volatility and are highly correlated among maturity classes and over various risk premiums, twists in the yield curve are rare and interest rate changes tend to be near-parallel shifts in the yield curve. Since duration-based measures of interest rate risk are best when there are small changes in interest rates and parallel shifts of the yield curve, they are poor measures when there are large changes in interest rates, with high volatility, and low correlation among interest rates associated with different maturities. These issues involving stochastic problems with interest rates and term structure generation are discussed more completely in Chapter 5.

Value-at-risk measures of interest rate risk take a different approach. They fix a maximum market price change having a 5 percent chance of occurring over the assumed period of time it would take to restructure the portfolio. The fundamental strength of this approach is that it attempts to account for interest rate volatility through the determination of an upper limit interest rate change. Otherwise, it too is a delta measure of interest rate risk, but for a chosen time period that may not be relevant to banking regulators.

One advantage of VaR over duration-based measurement is that it attempts to account for interest rate changes that are not simply parallel shifts of the yield curve. Through portfolio approaches to measure portfolio VaR, the correlation among interest rate changes is estimated and used to measure VaR. Since these correlations are estimated using historical movement—shifts and twists—of the yield curve, they permit the introduction of more complex interest rate changes than do parallel shifts. As we will discuss in Chapter 5, estimates of volatility and correlation are far from stable, and although their introduction in risk measurement allows more realistic portrayal of interest rate movements, volatility of correlations represents yet another source of risk.

The OTS measures suffer from the same deficiencies as the pure duration-based measures. However, they do attempt to measure optionality on mortgage-backed securities and to value interest rate options. But, the measurement remains strictly a delta measure of value changes and suffers from most of the same limitations as those of the banking agencies.

## Appendix

The estimation of the proportional change in price including convexity is accomplished using a Taylor expansion of the total proportional change in price and ignoring third- and higher-order terms:

$$\frac{dP}{P} = \frac{\partial P}{\partial ytm}\frac{1}{P}\,dytm + \frac{1}{2}\frac{\partial^2 P}{\partial ytm^2}\frac{1}{P}\,dytm^2 \qquad (A-1)$$

By multiplying the first term in equation (5) by $(1 + ytm)/(1 + ytm)$, this relationship can be converted into a duration-plus-convexity relationship:

$$\frac{dP}{P} = \frac{\partial P}{\partial ytm}\frac{1}{P}\,dytm\,\frac{(1 + ytm)}{(1 + ytm)} + \frac{1}{2}\frac{\partial^2 P}{\partial ytm^2}\frac{1}{P}\,dytm^2$$

$$(A-2)$$

$$= D_M\frac{dytm}{(1 + ytm)} + \frac{1}{2}\frac{\partial^2 P}{\partial ytm^2}\frac{1}{P}\,dytm^2$$

The second term in this relationship measures convexity times the square of the change in the yield to maturity. The convexity term is thus:

$$\text{Convexity} = \frac{1}{2} \frac{\partial^2 P}{\partial \text{ytm}^2} \frac{1}{P}$$

$$(A\text{--}3)$$

## The Change in Economic Value of Equity in Terms of Asset and Liability Changes

The agencies' proposal presents the change in the economic value of bank equity resulting from a change in interest rates as a proportion to the economic value of bank assets. It expresses this as the sum of interest rate risk weights for each asset, liability, and off–balance sheet item times the amount of each item divided by total assets. Conceptually, this model accounts for interest rate changes as they affect assets and liabilities (ignoring off–balance sheet items for simplicity) as a duration of assets and liabilities adjusted for the convexity in the value–interest rate relationship for each portfolio item. This is essentially a Taylor series expansion of each item with regard to a constant change in interest rates (as assumed by the parallel shift of the yield articulated in the banking agencies' proposal).

Defining the change in equity as the change in assets less the change in liabilities:

$$dE \equiv dA - dL = \sum_i^m dA_i - \sum_j^l dL_j$$

$$(A\text{--}4)$$

Using a Taylor expansion to approximate the change in each of the asset and liability elements with respect to a common change in interest rate and truncating all powers greater than the powers of 2:

$$\frac{dA_i}{A_i} = \left[ \frac{\partial A_i}{\partial y_i} \frac{dy_i}{A_i} A_i + \frac{1}{2} \frac{\partial^2 A_i}{\partial y_i^2} \frac{dy_i^2}{A_i} A_i \right]$$

$$\frac{dL_j}{L_j} = \left[ \frac{\partial L_j}{\partial y_j} \frac{dy_j}{L_j} L_j + \frac{1}{2} \frac{\partial^2 L_j}{\partial y_j^2} \frac{dy_j^2}{L_j} L_j \right]$$

$$(A\text{--}5)$$

The terms $dA_i/A_i$ and $dL_j/L_j$ are analogous (continuous equivalent) to the risk weights for each element as the proportional change in the economic value of the element with respect to the interest rate change. The change in equity as a proportion to assets (the banking agencies' net risk-weighted position to assets ratio) is found by substituting equations (A–5) into equation (A–4) and dividing through by total assets, $A$:

$$\frac{dE}{A} = \frac{1}{A}\sum_{i}^{m}\left[\frac{\partial A_i}{\partial y_i}\frac{dy_i}{A_i}A_i + \frac{1}{2}\frac{\partial^2 A_i}{\partial y_i^2}\frac{dy_i^2}{A_i}\right] - \frac{L}{A}\sum_{j}^{l}\left[\frac{\partial L_j}{\partial y_j}\frac{dy_j}{L_j}L_j + \frac{1}{2}\frac{\partial^2 L_j}{\partial y_j^2}\frac{dy_j^2}{L_j}L_j\right]\frac{1}{L} \qquad \text{(A–6)}$$

Essentially this relationship is the proportional change in assets less the leverage weight of the proportional change in liabilities due to interest rate changes—the banking agencies' interest rate risk exposure measure. This relationship can also be written in terms of the proportional change in the value of equity, as in equation (13) in the text.

The approach used in this appendix is to relate changes in bank equity value to the interest rate sensitivity of bank assets and liabilities. As in the simple model of the changes in bank equity presented in the text [equation (13)], the value of equity ($E$) of a bank is defined as the market value of assets ($A$) less the market value of liabilities ($L$), and assets are composed of separate investments (e.g., real property, loans) and liabilities are, likewise, composed of separate liability issues (e.g., CDs, subordinated debt, transactions accounts, etc.). The yield to maturity of each of these asset and liability elements may be different and represent different maturity or default risk characteristics. The interest sensitivity of each of these may also be different reflecting the terms of the asset or liability contract. In addition, the changes in interest rates may not be so perfectly correlated that a change in the 3-month T-bill rate will be the same as a change in the rate on 30-year mortgage yield. Thus, each element is likely to have associated with it a unique duration and convexity effect as well as a different market value trend over time (e.g., a zero-coupon bond will increase in market value as time to maturity decreases). These factors are assumed away by this approach, with the exception of different measures of duration, and suggest that measuring interest rate risk by this method is subject to some serious, but unknown, error that is not offset in aggregation over a portfolio.

# NOTES

1. Value at risk is a measurement of the largest effect on the value of an instrument or portfolio that could occur over a specified period (e.g., a day, week, or month) with a particular probability that value changes would not exceed this value (e.g., a 5 percent probability that over the specified period the value would not be exceeded).

2. The price of instruments with cash flows that vary precisely and directly with yield-to-maturity, that is, variable interest rate instruments will not demonstrate the inverse relationship, but will be virtually constant, all other factors the same.

3. Actually, if formula (2) is applied to coupon payments in 6-month intervals, the value of the computed duration should be divided by 2 to convert the $D_M$ measure to years (see Wood and Wood, 1985, pp. 148–60).

4. The slope is declining, such that the change in the slope (convexity) is negative—hence, the term negative convexity [see equation (6)].

5. See Gilkeson and Smith, 1993, pp. 150–56. In practical applications of pricing MBS with prepayment options, the technique of the "option-adjusted spread" is usually applied. For a discussion of this technique of adjusting the yield to maturity for the embedded option, see Stephen D. Smith, 1993, pp. 142 and 147–48.

6. The mortgage investor can fundamentally be thought of as shorting a series of interest rate put options ("floors") where the mortgage investor promises to pay (take a loss) when market interest rates go below the contract rate on the mortgage. The amount paid is the difference between the interest rate on the mortgage and the going market rate on a similar mortgage for the remaining maturity of the original mortgage. The value of the option represents a loss to the lender if interest rates fall below the contracted rate. The option is worthless if interest rates are above the contract rate, since the mortgagor will not exercise the option.

7. The value of the duration of a portfolio, like the duration of a single instrument, is in terms of time (years), and its sign is normally negative for banks due to the inverse relationship between the value of securities and the market yield to maturity. As is discussed below, the net effect of changes in asset value less changes in liability value due to changes in interest rates may give a positive sign if weighted liability duration exceeds asset duration, each with the convexity adjustment.

8. Economic value is the discounted cash flows expected from a particular asset, liability, or off–balance sheet item. By this definition, economic value need not necessarily equal market value, but is best

termed "fair" value. Market value and fair value are not always the same, because of many factors, one being expectations differences within the market and among investors. Notwithstanding these differences, the terms market value and fair value are used interchangeably throughout the text.

9. If the model were in terms of duration, it would be similar to the framework presented by George Kaufman (1984).

10. Recall that the values of $D_A$ and $D_L$ are each likely to be negative, so that, if assets have greater (more negative) modified duration than liabilities, it is likely that the net value for $dE/E$ is also negative.

11. For a more extensive discussion of portfolio convexity effects and hedging with duration, see Hugh Cohen (1993), pp. 23–24; and Gilkeson and Smith (1993), pp. 150–56.

12. Although the measure of VaR proposed by the Basle Agreement (1995 amendment) is a more general measure of changes in trading account value due to market risk from interest rates, foreign exchanges, and commodity prices, the proposal treats each source of risk as if it were independent within the overall portfolio of the firm. Thus, our analysis is consistent with Basle in focusing on interest rate risk independent of other sources of risk.

13. See J. P. Morgan *RiskMetrics* (1994, p. 82) for a discussion of using duration measures to approximate price volatility measures. Modified duration is Macaulay's duration divided by the current interest rate factor (1 + yield). By convention, yield changes are measured as the proportional change in yields so that the volatility estimate must be multiplied by the yield to convert it to a true yield change.

14. Refer to J. P. Morgan *RiskMetrics* (1994, p. 15) and Green and Mark (1994, pp. 728–29). The following is a more formal statement of the assumptions regarding stochastic properties:

    1. Relative price changes, returns, of individual financial assets are normally distributed with a constant variance, $\sigma$, and mean, $\mu$ (in some applications, the mean proportional change is assumed to be zero).

    2. Relative price changes are serially uncorrelated—returns in one period are uncorrelated with returns in any past or future periods.

    3. The parameters of the stochastic process generating returns are stable over time.

    4. The joint distribution of returns among assets of different maturities and other asset and commodity returns are joint normally distributed and characterized by stable, unserially correlated processes.

15. Note that the logarithmic difference approach would essentially be the difference in interest rates of a constant maturity zero-coupon security paying \$1 at $T$: $P_t = \exp(-y_t T)$ is the price of a zero-coupon security in period $t$ with a maturity of $T$ and a market yield of $y_t$. The logarithm of $P_t$ is $-y_t T$, and the logarithm of $P_{t-1}$ is $-y_{t-1}T$, so that the difference in the logarithms is $T(y_t - y_{t-1})$. This implies that the difference in interest rates on a one-period ($T = 1$) zero-coupon bond with constant maturity is assumed to be normally distributed. By convention, however, interest rate changes are measured in terms of relative changes, $\ln(y_t/y_{t-1})$, and their standard deviations are calculated accordingly.

16. The measure of duration could be enhanced by adding the correction for convexity, so that the duration measure would be duration plus convexity.

17. The data for this example are taken from J. P. Morgan, *RiskMetrics* (1994), pp. 9–11.

18. One position may be long while the other is short, or both may be long or short.

19. Refer to J. P. Morgan, *RiskMetrics* (1994, pp. 13–14), and Green and Mark (1994, pp. 729–30).

20. Operationally, measuring VaR for assets, liabilities, and off–balance sheet items will be taken up in Chapter 5 in the full discussion of estimation of volatilities and correlations.

## REFERENCES

Basle Committee on Banking Supervision, "Planned Supplement to the Capital Accord to Incorporate Market Risks," Bank for International Settlements, Basle Switzerland, April 1995.

Bierwag, Gerald O. *Duration Analysis: Managing Interest Rate Risk.* Cambridge, MA: Ballinger, 1987.

Bierwag, G. O., George G. Kaufman, and Alden L. Toevs. "Single Factor Duration Models in a Discrete General Equilibrium Framework," *Journal of Finance* 37 (May 1982), pp. 105–57.

Cohen, Hugh. "Beyond Duration: Measuring Interest Rate Exposure," *Economic Review* 78 (March–April 1993), Federal Reserve Bank of Atlanta, pp. 23–31.

Fabozzi, Frank J. *Bond Markets, Analysis and Strategies.* 2nd ed. Englewood Cliffs, NJ: Prentice Hall, 1993.

Federal Reserve Board, Press Release, *Interagency Advanced Notice of Proposed Rulemaking to Revise Risk-Based Capital Standards*, July 30, 1992.

Federal Reserve Board, "Press Release on 'Prompt Corrective Action'," September 18, 1992.

Federal Reserve Board, Press Release, *Interagency Notice of Proposed Rulemaking to Revise Risk-Based Capital Standards*, September 14, 1993.

Fisher, Lawrence, and Roman L. Weil. "Coping with the Risk of Interest-Rate Fluctuations: Returns to Bondholders from Naive and Optimal Strategies," *Journal of Business* 44 (October 1971), pp. 408–31.

Gilkeson, James H., and Stephen D. Smith. "The Convexity Trap: Pitfalls in Financing Mortgage Portfolios and Related Securities," in *Financial Derivatives: New Instruments and Their Uses*, Federal Reserve Bank of Atlanta, 1993, pp. 150–64.

Green, Henry, and Robert Mark. "Managing Portfolio Positions," In *The Handbook of Interest Rate Risk Management*, ed. Jack Clark Francis and Avner Wolf. Burr Ridge, IL: Irwin Professional Publishing, 1994, pp. 717–736.

———— and ————. "Prudential Supervision to Manage Systematic Vulnerability," *Proceedings of a Conference on Bank Structure and Competition*, Federal Reserve Bank of Chicago, 1988, p. 602.

Kaufman, George G. "Measuring and Managing Interest Rate Risk: A Primer," Federal Reserve Bank of Chicago, *Economic Perspectives* 8 (January–February 1984), pp. 16–26.

Macaulay, Frederick R. *The Movements of Interest Rates, Bond Yields and Stock Prices in the United States Since 1856*, New York, NY, National Bureau of Economic Research, 1938.

Morgan, J. P., *RiskMetrics*, J. P. Morgan & Co., New York, NY, October 1994.

Smith, Stephen D. "Analyzing Risk and Return for Mortgage-Backed Securities," in *Financial Derivatives: New Instruments and Their Uses*, Federal Reserve Bank of Atlanta, 1993, pp. 139–149.

Toevs, Alden. "Gap Management: Managing Interest Rate Risk in Banks and Thrifts," Federal Reserve Bank of San Francisco *Economic Review* (Spring 1983).

Wood, John H., and Norma L. Wood. *Financial Markets*. New York: Harcourt Brace Jovanovich, 1985.

Wriston, Walter B. "Bank Weaknesses Are a Regulatory Illusion," *The Wall Street Journal*, February 7, 1992.

*Chapter Five*

# Modeling the Impact of Interest Rate Risk

As noted already, two choices need to be made by banks and by the federal banking agencies in evaluating interest rate risk. The first is a choice of technique for measuring the effects of changes in interest rates on the value of financial instruments; alternative methodologies were presented in Chapter 4. The second is a choice of technique to determine the effects of interest rate changes on the market value of a bank's portfolio or net worth. These "modeling" techniques or methodologies are reviewed and evaluated in this chapter.

## MODELING METHODOLOGIES: THE FEDERAL BANKING AGENCIES' APPROACH

As in the case of measurement, there are a number of modeling methodologies that yield results that differ in important ways. We begin with a review and evaluation of the federal banking agencies' approach to finesse the intrinsically complex problem of determining interest rate risk and leveling a capital charge for excessive exposure without overburdening banks. We then develop some other techniques that we view as preferable.

### Evaluation of Interest Rate Risk under the Agencies' Proposal

Federal agency proposals, required by FDICIA (Section 305), have been motivated by recognition that risk-based capital requirements and "prompt corrective action" (Section 131) may be insufficient to protect the federal deposit insurance fund in the face of interest rate changes that reduce bank equity value.[1] The agency proposal in 1993 developed a method for determining the additions to capital necessary to meet "excessive" interest rate risk, as measured by a newly developed index (IRR index). It accomplished this by converting interest rate risk into a comparable increase in risk-adjusted assets and, therefore, credit risk.[2]

A recent proposal by the agencies (August 1995) requires banks to report interest rate risk exposure through the use of either an agency-prescribed model or a bank's own model (internal model) approved by the agencies. But it abandons the effort to provide a systematic transformation of excessive interest rate risk into additions to risk-based capital requirements. Nevertheless, because banks can substitute interest rate risk for credit risk, the agencies still find it necessary to impose capital assessments for excessive exposure. The proposal simply indicates that interest rate risk exposure, as measured, will be evaluated by examiners who, in their discretion, will determine whether or not capital is adequate.

## The Agencies' Interest Rate Sensitivity Model

The proposed regulatory interest rate index, or IRR, developed in the agencies' 1993 proposal, is defined as the total change in the value of bank equity, relative to the value of assets, resulting from interest rate changes. The basic relationship is shown in Chapter 4 as equation (13). That equation can be rewritten so that the change in equity is divided by assets, rather than equity:[3]

$$\text{IRR} = \frac{dE}{A} = \frac{1}{A}\left[\frac{\partial A}{\partial y_A}\,dy_A + \frac{1}{2}\frac{\partial^2 A}{\partial y_A^2}\,dy_A^2\right] - \frac{1}{L}\left[\frac{\partial L}{\partial y_L}\,dy_L + \frac{1}{2}\frac{\partial^2 L}{\partial y_L^2}\,dy_L^2\right]\frac{L}{A} \qquad (1)$$

The proposal evaluates interest rate risk on the basis of an equal change in yield for all assets and liabilities—a ±200 bp parallel shift of the yield curve for all risk classes. In equation (1), showing the relationship between interest rate risk and interest rate changes, a parallel shift means that interest rate changes, $dy$, are assumed to be the same for each asset and liability. The proposal also assumes that the proportional change in asset value (for each asset) and liability value (for each liability) depends only on the mix of assets and liabilities and is constant over time and independent of their volume. To determine the impact on equity, it postulates a uniform interest rate change (shock) that does not vary over time. As a result, $dy_A$ is equal to $dy_L$ in equation (1). These assumptions permit the IRR index to be simplified as follows:

$$\text{IRR} = \frac{dE}{A} = \left[\lambda_A - \lambda_L \frac{L}{A}\right] dy \tag{2}$$

where, $\lambda_j dy$ is the proportional change in assets or liabilities due to interest rate changes.[4] These values are each likely to be negative. The value in brackets will also be negative, since $L/A$ is 1.0 or less.

This relationship shows that as a bank increases its equity relative to assets—that is, as the liability-to-asset ratio falls—the IRR index (IRR) becomes more negative for any given interest rate increase. This is because, in the formulation, the proportional decline in asset values becomes increasingly more important relative to the proportional increase in liability values. In the extreme case, where a bank has no liabilities, $\lambda_L$ is negative, and the bank's assets are supported by equity alone (the liability-to-asset ratio $L/A$ becomes zero), the index reaches its lowest possible value. This minimum value is the proportional change in the market value of the bank's assets resulting from a change in interest rates ($\lambda_A dy$). The disconcerting implication is that additions to capital prompted by excess interest rate risk will *worsen* the IRR index. Were examiners to consider the index alone, it would prompt them to ask for more capital to sustain any given risk-based capital levels as equity is increased.

### A Hypothetical Example Using the Agencies' Model

Using hypothetical bank data presented in the July 1995 agency proposal, a numerical example can be constructed to illustrate that, as computed by the model, increases in equity will serve only to worsen the IRR index. Table 5–1 shows the effect of an interest rate increase of +200 bp; Figure 5–1 graphs the relationship between the relative change in equity to assets and the IRR index. It can be seen in Figure 5–1 how increases in equity to assets serve to increase the index. It is an anomaly that banks with less leverage, holding asset and liability composition constant, will have IRR indexes indicating a greater exposure to interest rate risk than banks with more leverage.

**TABLE 5–1**

*Relationship of IRR and Convexity Adjusted Equity Changes to Leverage*

| IRR Index (%) (dy = 200bp) | E/A | L/A | $\lambda_A dy$ (%) | $\lambda_L dy$ (%) | $\Delta E/E$ (%) |
|---|---|---|---|---|---|
| 2.679 | 0.102 | 0.898 | 4.941 | 2.418 | 27.114 |
| 2.727 | 0.122 | 0.878 | 4.941 | 2.418 | 23.071 |
| 2.775 | 0.142 | 0.858 | 4.941 | 2.418 | 20.165 |
| 2.824 | 0.162 | 0.838 | 4.941 | 2.418 | 17.976 |
| 2.872 | 0.182 | 0.818 | 4.941 | 2.418 | 16.268 |
| 2.920 | 0.202 | 0.798 | 4.941 | 2.418 | 14.898 |
| 2.969 | 0.222 | 0.778 | 4.941 | 2.418 | 13.774 |
| 3.017 | 0.242 | 0.758 | 4.941 | 2.418 | 12.836 |
| 3.065 | 0.262 | 0.738 | 4.941 | 2.418 | 12.042 |
| 3.114 | 0.282 | 0.718 | 4.941 | 2.418 | 11.359 |
| 3.162 | 0.302 | 0.698 | 4.941 | 2.418 | 10.768 |
| 3.210 | 0.322 | 0.678 | 4.941 | 2.418 | 10.249 |
| 3.259 | 0.342 | 0.658 | 4.941 | 2.418 | 9.791 |
| 3.307 | 0.362 | 0.638 | 4.941 | 2.418 | 9.384 |
| 3.356 | 0.382 | 0.618 | 4.941 | 2.418 | 9.020 |
| 3.404 | 0.402 | 0.598 | 4.941 | 2.418 | 8.691 |
| 3.452 | 0.422 | 0.578 | 4.941 | 2.418 | 8.394 |
| 3.501 | 0.442 | 0.558 | 4.941 | 2.418 | 8.124 |
| 3.549 | 0.462 | 0.538 | 4.941 | 2.418 | 7.877 |
| 3.597 | 0.482 | 0.518 | 4.941 | 2.418 | 7.650 |
| 3.646 | 0.502 | 0.498 | 4.941 | 2.418 | 7.442 |
| 3.694 | 0.522 | 0.478 | 4.941 | 2.418 | 7.250 |
| 3.742 | 0.542 | 0.458 | 4.941 | 2.418 | 7.071 |
| 3.791 | 0.562 | 0.438 | 4.941 | 2.418 | 6.906 |
| 3.839 | 0.582 | 0.418 | 4.941 | 2.418 | 6.752 |
| 3.887 | 0.602 | 0.398 | 4.941 | 2.418 | 6.608 |
| 3.936 | 0.622 | 0.378 | 4.941 | 2.418 | 6.473 |
| 3.984 | 0.642 | 0.358 | 4.941 | 2.418 | 6.347 |
| 4.033 | 0.662 | 0.338 | 4.941 | 2.418 | 6.228 |
| 4.081 | 0.682 | 0.318 | 4.941 | 2.418 | 6.116 |
| 4.129 | 0.702 | 0.298 | 4.941 | 2.418 | 6.011 |
| 4.178 | 0.722 | 0.278 | 4.941 | 2.418 | 5.912 |
| 4.226 | 0.742 | 0.258 | 4.941 | 2.418 | 5.817 |
| 4.274 | 0.762 | 0.238 | 4.941 | 2.418 | 5.728 |
| 4.323 | 0.782 | 0.218 | 4.941 | 2.418 | 5.644 |

*continued*

**TABLE 5–1—*Continued***
*Relationship of IRR and Convexity Adjusted Equity Changes to Leverage*

| IRR Index (%)<br>(dy = 200bp) | E/A | L/A | $\lambda_A dy$<br>(%) | $\lambda_L dy$<br>(%) | $\Delta E/E$ (%) |
|---|---|---|---|---|---|
| 4.371 | 0.802 | 0.198 | 4.941 | 2.418 | 5.563 |
| 4.419 | 0.822 | 0.178 | 4.941 | 2.418 | 5.487 |
| 4.468 | 0.842 | 0.158 | 4.941 | 2.418 | 5.414 |
| 4.516 | 0.862 | 0.138 | 4.941 | 2.418 | 5.344 |
| 4.565 | 0.882 | 0.118 | 4.941 | 2.418 | 5.278 |
| 4.613 | 0.902 | 0.098 | 4.941 | 2.418 | 5.214 |
| 4.661 | 0.922 | 0.078 | 4.941 | 2.418 | 5.154 |
| 4.710 | 0.942 | 0.058 | 4.941 | 2.418 | 5.096 |
| 4.758 | 0.962 | 0.038 | 4.941 | 2.418 | 5.040 |
| 4.806 | 0.982 | 0.018 | 4.941 | 2.418 | 4.987 |
| 4.849 | 1.000 | 0.000 | 4.941 | 2.418 | 4.941 |

Source: Federal Reserve Board Release September 14, 1993, Table 2, p. 55

**FIGURE 5–1**
*IRR and the Convexity-Adjusted Change in Equity ($\Delta E/E$) As Related to Equity to Assets (E/A) (dy = 200 bp)*

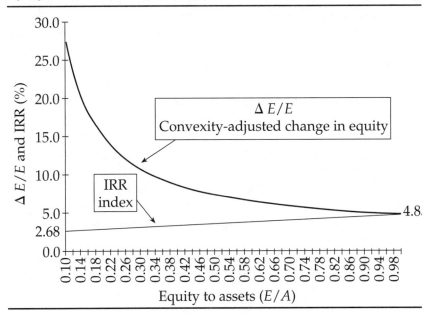

Source: Federal Reserve Board Release September 14, 1993, Table 2, p. 55.

The example shows an initial IRR index (the ratio of net risk-weighted position to assets) of –2.678 percent.[5] If the bank desired to account for this degree of interest rate risk so as to keep its risk-based capital ratio constant, it would need to add capital to cover its exposure. If it considered excess exposure as an index above 1.0 percent, as had been proposed by the agencies, it would need to add capital in an amount equal to 1.678 percent of its total assets, or $3.121 million. Assuming no change in the composition of assets and liabilities, and that total assets remain constant, the required capital addition will raise the equity-to-asset ratio from 10.22 percent to 11.89 percent, and *raise* (make more negative) the IRR index from –2.678 to –2.719 percent.

An increase in the IRR index after the addition of capital might suggest that the bank should have increased its equity by more than the 1.678 percent of assets initially required. But doing so would only have increased its IRR index further. *Increases in equity will never permit the bank to reach the threshold of 1.0 percent.* An all equity bank would have an index, or net risk-weighted position, of –4.85 percent (see Figure 5–1).[6] Continuing to add capital, in accordance with the proposed rule, continues to raise the bank's capital-to-asset ratio until the bank's liabilities relative to its capital become inconsequential and the IRR index approximates –4.85 percent, for a +200 bp interest rate increase.[7]

An interesting implication of the IRR index, in the category of unintended regulatory effects, is that its use by the agencies would alter bank incentives in their asset-liability management. Because the index increases with additions to equity, without any apparent change risk, those banks identified as excessively exposed can only reduce their measured exposure (reach the IRR threshold established) by altering the structural characteristics of their portfolios—in particular, by reducing the duration of assets and/or increasing the duration of liabilities and/or hedging in off–balance sheet items. Even a bank that increases its equity to become "adequately capitalized" or "well capitalized" within the provisions of FDICIA's "prompt corrective action" provisions will find its IRR index worsening.

In contrast, the convexity-adjusted proportional change in equity, $\Delta E/E$, shown with the index in Figure 5–1, declines (becomes less negative) as equity is added. It shows that capital additions can reduce interest rate risk, but that there is a lower limit given by the composition of assets and their convexity-adjusted duration.

Additions to capital do provide the insurance fund with additional protection. But they are, at best, limited in their effectiveness in modifying the exposure of banks to interest rate risk. The IRR index as an indicator of needed capital is, moreover, misleading and counterproductive. It potentially would impose a double cost on banks: the cost of increased capital, and the cost incurred in finding other mechanisms that are effective in protecting against the interest rate risk it purports to measure.

### Measuring the Interest Rate Risk of
### Off–Balance Sheet Derivatives

Before developing alternatives to the agencies' model, it is useful to note that certain off–balance sheet items need to be considered in all models. Most derivative instruments used by banks, including forward and futures contracts and interest rate swaps, are not recorded as either assets or liabilities, but reported as off–balance sheet items. Some have changes in value that move only in a single direction with changes in interest rates. For example, the values of interest rate forward and futures contracts will decrease with an increase in interest rates for a long position and increase with a short position. Other types of derivative contracts have more complex relationships with interest rate changes. Banks can achieve more efficient portfolios at lower costs by using these contracts to manage interest rate, foreign exchange, and other market risks. Some examples of how this is done are presented below.

## ALTERNATIVE APPROACHES

Criticism of the agency proposal is not meant to suggest that guidelines or requirements for protection against interest rate risk are unnecessary. Its defects require, however, that alternative approaches be considered. Throughout the analysis below, we recognize that the efficient use of hedging instruments is an appropriate substitute for increased capital and that the use of these instruments will require an aggressive examiner and banker education effort.[8]

## An Alternative Static Measure of Interest Rate Risk Exposure

The agencies' model can be considered "static" in the sense that it postulates a one-time change in interest rates (200 basis points) and computes the effects on bank value without any consideration of time over which the rate change and its effects occur. A preferable static measure of bank interest rate risk exposure can be developed that better accounts for differences in interest rates among assets and liabilities, and better defines the relationship of interest rate risk to changes in equity capital and leverage.[9]

The agencies' model presented in equation (1) can be elaborated to develop a measure that indicates the effect of a change in the opportunity cost of equity $(1 + y_j)$ on equity value—what might be called a "total elasticity" measure, in that it indicates the proportional or percentage changes in equity values resulting from small changes in interest rates. Beginning with equation (2) above, and recalling that the proportional change in assets or liabilities due to a change in interest rates is denoted as the product of $\lambda_j$ and $dy$, elasticities for assets and liabilities may be calculated as follows (see Appendix A of this chapter for the derivation):

$$\frac{dE}{A} = \left[ \frac{(1 + y_L)\, \xi_A - (1 + y_A)\, \xi_L}{(1 + y_L)(1 + y_A)} \frac{L}{A} \right] dy \tag{3}$$

Expressing this relationship in terms of the proportional change in the economic value of equity with respect to a change in interest rates and assuming that the yield on assets $y_A$ is the opportunity cost of equity results in the following (a derivation of the formula is provided in Appendix A to this chapter):

$$\frac{dE}{E} \frac{(1 + y_A)}{dy} = \xi_E = \left[ \xi_A - \frac{(1 + y_A)\, \xi_L}{(1 + y_L)} \frac{L}{A} \right] \frac{A}{E} \tag{4}$$

Equation (4) indicates that when we hold constant the composition of assets, liabilities, and off–balance sheet items, the elasticity of equity $(\xi_E)$ increases (becomes less negative) as equity is increased and leverage is reduced. In the extreme case of an all-equity bank, the elasticity of equity approaches the elasticity of assets ($\xi_A$). In this sense, the result is comparable to the agencies' model. The lowest possible value for interest rate risk exposure that a bank can achieve is determined by the elasticity of assets. Again, there is an important lower limit that a bank can alter only by changing its assets, liabilities, and/or off–balance sheet activities.

The elasticity measure is, nevertheless, preferable to the agencies' model because it is sensitive to the relative levels of interest rates on assets and liabilities from which the 200 basis point shock emerges. This sensitivity is reflected in the ratio of $(1 + y_A)$ to $(1 + y_L)$. In contrast, the agencies' IRR index ignores relationships between the rates on assets and liabilities.

Assuming asset yields are associated with longer maturities than liability yields, a narrowing of the spread between these rate factors, which may be interpreted as a flattening of the yield curve, results in the equity–interest rate elasticity becoming more negative, indicating greater interest rate sensitivity of equity to interest rate changes and greater interest rate risk for the same portfolio composition. But the agencies' IRR measure does not take into consideration changes in the shape of the yield curve, a common condition that should not be ignored.

The elasticity measure, then, should provide a better evaluation of interest rate risk exposure than the agencies' model. It requires the same information, and it has readily determined threshold values that can be calculated for banks and that can be easily interpreted by bankers and examiners. If the agencies must use a static model of interest rate risk exposure, they would be better advised to use the elasticity measure.

## A Stochastic Measure of Interest Rate Risk Exposure and Historical Interest Rate Volatility

All static interest rate risk measures are, however, deficient. In the real world, the levels of interest rates change over time, interest rate volatilities change, and yield curves twist. As a result, these measures cannot accurately measure the potential changes in equity. The volatility of interest rates is usually greater for shorter- than for longer-maturity instruments and will depend upon the level of interest rates and the shape of the yield curve, which in turn will reflect the monetary policy restraint and objectives, and general economic conditions.[10] Because different portfolios are characterized by different maturities, at any point in time, they will also be characterized by different exposures. Because the level and shape of the yield curve change over time, the exposure of any given portfolio will also change.

In general, the higher the volatility of the yields or rates on the assets and liabilities in a bank's portfolio, the greater will be the bank's exposure to interest rate risk; that is, the greater will be the expected volatility in the value of its equity. Banks may have the same static IRR index, or "elasticity of equity," and still be differentially exposed to interest rate risk because they have differently sensitive portfolios.[11] In large measure, the extent of a bank's sensitivity is an empirical question that requires a dynamic and stochastic (probabilistic) approach to measuring exposure.

In addition to the measurement of equity changes in response to interest rate changes, the stochastic approach requires a determination of the likelihood of changes in interest rate levels and volatilities. Measurement can be based on historical information about the volatility of interest rates, particularly with regard to the asset-liability structure of the bank. By considering the stochastic processes affecting interest rates at different maturities, a better determination can be made of the likely impact on a bank's equity and any likelihood that it will be significantly reduced.

In order to approach this problem of stochastic effects on bank equity, we introduce a stochastic model that is developed in Appendix B of this chapter. For reference, we reproduce equation B–12 from Appendix B:

$$\frac{dE(Y,t)}{E} = \frac{A}{E} \sum_i \frac{w_i D_i}{(1 + y_i)} \sigma_i(y_i, t) \, dz + \frac{\partial E}{\partial t} \frac{dt}{E} + \frac{1}{2} \sum_i \sum_j \sigma_{ij} \frac{\partial^2 E}{\partial y_i \, \partial y_j} \frac{dt}{E} \quad (5)$$

Referring to equation (5), it is clear that a probable (stochastic) change in the value of bank equity will depend on several factors. These include (1) the level of interest rates ($y_i$); (2) the duration of asset and liability value from an interest rate change ($D_i$); (3) the standard deviation of interest rate changes ($\sigma_i$ and $\sigma_{ij}$ when $i = j$); and (4) the covariance among interest rate changes of assets and liabilities ($\sigma_{ij}$). The $dz_i$ terms represent normally distributed, independent random variables that have zero mean and a variance that is a constant proportion of the time interval between changes and not on specific dates (generally known as Wiener processes).

The complex final term in equation (5) includes an element similar to the convexity term of equations (5) and (6) in Chapter 4, $\left(\dfrac{1}{2}\dfrac{\partial^2 E}{\partial\text{ytm}^2}\dfrac{1}{E}\right)$. The sign of the convexity element is expected to be positive. The sign of the entire term, however, will depend upon the sign of the covariances. As shown below, covariances among interest rate changes by different maturities are positive for Treasury securities.

The stochastic relationship indicates that the standard deviations and covariances of interest rate changes are critical to evaluating interest rate risk. Even with convexity and covariance constant, a rise in interest volatility (reflected in an increase in the standard deviation) can raise expected exposure to interest rate risk, that is, the sensitivity of equity to any given interest rate change. However, a rise in one interest rate may indicate a rise in all others (positive covariances) such that a positive convexity may dampen any negative effects on equity values. Additionally, by taking the expected value of equation (5) and noting that for a Wiener process the expected value of $dz_i$ is zero [$E(dz_i) = 0$], a rise in both volatility and covariance will increase the expected value of equity changes. A realistic evaluation of the effect of interest rate changes on bank equity values requires an understanding of how the yield curve changes in periods of different interest rate volatilities, that is, historical information on different interest rate volatility "regimes."

The federal banking agencies' proposal evaluates historical experience in terms of a simplifying assumption. It treats interest rate volatility and covariances as constant parameters to be estimated from historical data, implying that means, standard deviations, and covariances of interest rate changes affecting bank assets and liabilities are time-invariant and stationary.[12]

The estimated values to predict future variances and covariances, as well as the joint probability distributions of interest rate changes for bank assets and liabilities, are not, however, realistic because the underlying assumption is not realistic. Interest rates have exhibited regimes of high volatility and low volatility.[13]

Figure 5–2 presents the 13-week T-bill weekly auction yield, $r(13:t)$, from 1960:1 to 1993:30 (the solid line) and the probability of being in a high-volatility interest rate regime (the "spiked" lines and left axis). The dark bars represent recession periods from cyclical peak to trough as identified by the National Bureau of Economic Research.[14]

The expectations hypothesis with a term premium is supported during periods of low volatility for short-term yields, but these relationships using the implied forward rate, derived from relationships between the 13-week and 26-week T-bill yields, become unstable during periods of high volatility.[15] Support is found for the hypothesis that the variance of interest rate changes over the entire term structure is greater during periods of high interest rate volatility, as measured by changes in the 13-week T-bill rate, than during periods of low volatility (Table 5–2).[16] These data also show that in low-volatility regimes, the standard deviation of interest rates over all maturity classes is virtually constant for each of the time periods. The result is remarkably different in high-volatility regimes, where the standard deviation of interest rate changes declines as maturity increases from 0.77 percent for 13-week T-bills to 0.26 percent for the 30-year T-bond (Table 5–2, both panels, 1977–1993 period).

As discussed in detail in Hanweck and Hanweck (1993), interest rate volatility is higher. That is, the variance in interest rate changes is greater and more statistically significant from zero during periods of recession and periods of falling interest rates. The high-volatility regimes are not predictable, but contribute significantly to explaining interest rate term premium changes, and, as suggested below, they help explain shifts of the term structure (Hanweck and Hanweck, 1993).

As further evidence that the characteristic movements of interest rates are different during periods of high- and low-volatility regimes, correlations of interest rate changes among maturities of Treasury securities were computed (Tables 5–3 and 5–4). For all time periods, correlations among interest rate changes on a weekly basis are positive. The correlations tend to be higher during high-volatility regimes and decline with maturities farther out on the yield curve. Correspondingly, interest rate changes of near maturities tend to be more highly correlated. Referring to

# FIGURE 5-2
*Recessions, High-Volatility Regime Probabilities, and*
*13-Week T-Bill Rates*

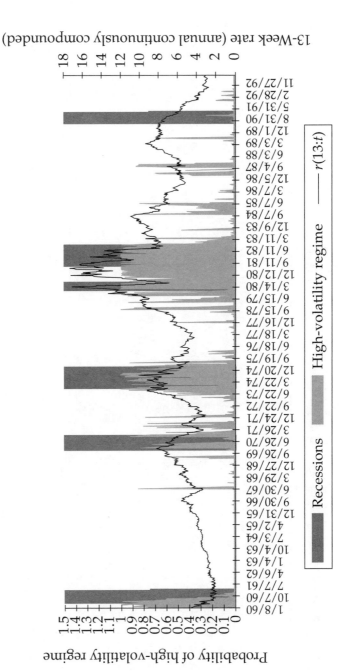

## TABLE 5–2
### Volatility of Changes in Treasury Security Yields By Maturity in High- and Low-Volatility Regimes*
(Weekly Changes %/yr)

Period 1977–93

| Maturity | 3 Mo | 6 Mo | 1 Yr | 2 Yr | 3 Yr | 5 Yr | 7 Yr | 10 Yr | 30 Yr |
|---|---|---|---|---|---|---|---|---|---|
| Variance high | 0.5977 | 0.4674 | 0.2504 | 0.1872 | 0.1511 | 0.1233 | 0.1034 | 0.0892 | 0.0681 |
| Standard deviation high | 0.7731 | 0.6836 | 0.5004 | 0.4327 | 0.3887 | 0.3511 | 0.3216 | 0.2986 | 0.2609 |
| Observations high | 205.0000 | 205.0000 | 205.0000 | 205.0000 | 205.0000 | 205.0000 | 205.0000 | 205.0000 | 205.0000 |
| Variance low | 0.0192 | 0.0201 | 0.0199 | 0.0200 | 0.0205 | 0.0227 | 0.0185 | 0.0173 | 0.0142 |
| Standard deviation low | 0.1386 | 0.1418 | 0.1410 | 0.1413 | 0.1432 | 0.1506 | 0.1359 | 0.1315 | 0.1191 |
| Observations low | 670 | 670 | 670 | 670 | 670 | 670 | 670 | 670 | 670 |
| f-stastic | 31.1047 | 23.2372 | 12.5921 | 9.3719 | 7.3710 | 5.4373 | 5.6051 | 5.1581 | 4.7982 |

Period 1962–93

| Maturity | 3 Mo | 6 Mo | 1 Yr | 3 Yr | 5 Yr | 10 Yr |
|---|---|---|---|---|---|---|
| Variance high | 0.4976 | 0.3892 | 0.1934 | 0.1157 | 0.0942 | 0.0654 |
| Standard deviation high | 0.7048 | 0.6230 | 0.4403 | 0.3407 | 0.3074 | 0.2562 |
| Observations high | 299.0000 | 299.0000 | 299.0000 | 299.0000 | 299.0000 | 299.0000 |
| Variance low | 0.0176 | 0.0208 | 0.0169 | 0.0160 | 0.0154 | 0.0114 |
| Standard deviation low | 0.1325 | 0.1441 | 0.1300 | 0.1265 | 0.1243 | 0.1068 |
| Observations low | 1365 | 1365 | 1365 | 1365 | 1365 | 1365 |
| f-stastic | 28.3447 | 18.7487 | 11.4517 | 7.2379 | 6.1008 | 5.7441 |

*All variances for high-volatility regimes are statistically greater for all maturities and time periods.

Source: Federal Reserve, H15 Releases and database for various years.

**TABLE 5–3**
*Correlations of Interest Changes by Maturity*
U.S. Treasury Securities (Period 2/18/77–11/26/93)

|        | 3 Mo | 6 Mo | 1 Yr | 2 Yr | 3 Yr | 5 Yr | 7 Yr | 10 Yr | 30 Yr |
|--------|------|------|------|------|------|------|------|-------|-------|
| *All*  |      | N = 875 |   |      |      |      |      |       |       |
| 3 mo   | 1.00 |      |      |      |      |      |      |       |       |
| 6 mo   | 0.93 | 1.00 |      |      |      |      |      |       |       |
| 1 yr   | 0.66 | 0.74 | 1.00 |      |      |      |      |       |       |
| 2 yr   | 0.63 | 0.71 | 0.97 | 1.00 |      |      |      |       |       |
| 3 yr   | 0.59 | 0.68 | 0.94 | 0.98 | 1.00 |      |      |       |       |
| 5 yr   | 0.53 | 0.62 | 0.88 | 0.92 | 0.95 | 1.00 |      |       |       |
| 7 yr   | 0.51 | 0.61 | 0.86 | 0.92 | 0.95 | 0.96 | 1.00 |       |       |
| 10 yr  | 0.50 | 0.59 | 0.84 | 0.89 | 0.93 | 0.94 | 0.99 | 1.00  |       |
| 30 yr  | 0.48 | 0.56 | 0.79 | 0.84 | 0.87 | 0.89 | 0.94 | 0.96  | 1.00  |
| *Expansion* |  | N = 732 |  |      |      |      |      |       |       |
| 3 mo   | 1.00 |      |      |      |      |      |      |       |       |
| 6 mo   | 0.93 | 1.00 |      |      |      |      |      |       |       |
| 1 yr   | 0.59 | 0.67 | 1.00 |      |      |      |      |       |       |
| 2 yr   | 0.58 | 0.66 | 0.96 | 1.00 |      |      |      |       |       |
| 3 yr   | 0.53 | 0.63 | 0.93 | 0.98 | 1.00 |      |      |       |       |
| 5 yr   | 0.46 | 0.56 | 0.84 | 0.90 | 0.93 | 1.00 |      |       |       |
| 7 yr   | 0.47 | 0.58 | 0.85 | 0.91 | 0.95 | 0.94 | 1.00 |       |       |
| 10 yr  | 0.46 | 0.56 | 0.81 | 0.88 | 0.92 | 0.92 | 0.98 | 1.00  |       |
| 30 yr  | 0.44 | 0.53 | 0.76 | 0.82 | 0.86 | 0.86 | 0.94 | 0.97  | 1.00  |
| *Recession* |  | N = 143 |  |      |      |      |      |       |       |
| 3 mo   | 1.00 |      |      |      |      |      |      |       |       |
| 6 mo   | 0.93 | 1.00 |      |      |      |      |      |       |       |
| 1 yr   | 0.73 | 0.81 | 1.00 |      |      |      |      |       |       |
| 2 yr   | 0.68 | 0.76 | 0.98 | 1.00 |      |      |      |       |       |
| 3 yr   | 0.66 | 0.74 | 0.95 | 0.98 | 1.00 |      |      |       |       |
| 5 yr   | 0.62 | 0.70 | 0.92 | 0.95 | 0.97 | 1.00 |      |       |       |
| 7 yr   | 0.56 | 0.64 | 0.88 | 0.92 | 0.95 | 0.99 | 1.00 |       |       |
| 10 yr  | 0.54 | 0.63 | 0.87 | 0.91 | 0.94 | 0.97 | 0.99 | 1.00  |       |
| 30 yr  | 0.53 | 0.59 | 0.82 | 0.85 | 0.89 | 0.92 | 0.95 | 0.96  | 1.00  |

*continued*

**TABLE 5–3—Continued**
*Correlations of Interest Changes by Maturity*
*U.S. Treasury Securities (Period 2/18/77–11/26/93)*

|            | 3 Mo | 6 Mo | 1 Yr | 2 Yr | 3 Yr | 5 Yr | 7 Yr | 10 Yr | 30 Yr |
|------------|------|------|------|------|------|------|------|-------|-------|
| *Low Variance* | *N = 670* | | | | | | | | |
| 3 mo  | 1.00 | | | | | | | | |
| 6 mo  | 0.87 | 1.00 | | | | | | | |
| 1 yr  | 0.54 | 0.66 | 1.00 | | | | | | |
| 2 yr  | 0.50 | 0.65 | 0.95 | 1.00 | | | | | |
| 3 yr  | 0.46 | 0.62 | 0.92 | 0.97 | 1.00 | | | | |
| 5 yr  | 0.40 | 0.54 | 0.81 | 0.88 | 0.90 | 1.00 | | | |
| 7 yr  | 0.40 | 0.56 | 0.84 | 0.91 | 0.94 | 0.92 | 1.00 | | |
| 10 yr | 0.38 | 0.54 | 0.81 | 0.88 | 0.92 | 0.90 | 0.99 | 1.00 | |
| 30 yr | 0.33 | 0.48 | 0.75 | 0.81 | 0.85 | 0.84 | 0.94 | 0.96 | 1.00 |
| *High Variance* | *N = 205* | | | | | | | | |
| 3 mo  | 1.00 | | | | | | | | |
| 6 mo  | 0.94 | 1.00 | | | | | | | |
| 1 yr  | 0.69 | 0.76 | 1.00 | | | | | | |
| 2 yr  | 0.67 | 0.74 | 0.98 | 1.00 | | | | | |
| 3 yr  | 0.65 | 0.72 | 0.95 | 0.98 | 1.00 | | | | |
| 5 yr  | 0.60 | 0.68 | 0.92 | 0.96 | 0.97 | 1.00 | | | |
| 7 yr  | 0.58 | 0.65 | 0.89 | 0.93 | 0.95 | 0.99 | 1.00 | | |
| 10 yr | 0.57 | 0.65 | 0.87 | 0.91 | 0.94 | 0.97 | 0.99 | 1.00 | |
| 30 yr | 0.57 | 0.63 | 0.83 | 0.86 | 0.89 | 0.92 | 0.95 | 0.97 | 1.00 |

Source: Federal Reserve, H15 Releases and database for various years.

Table 5–3 and the high-variance panel, correlations with the 3-month T-bill decline from 0.94 with the 6-month T-bill to 0.57 with the 30-year T-bond. In contrast, viewing the same panel for the 30-year T-bond, the correlation increases to 0.97 with the 10-year T-bond.

These findings imply that identification of the volatility regime is fundamental to being able to confidently predict (or project) the effect of interest rate changes on the economic value of a bank. In working with equation (5), we are obliged to conclude that:

1. High-volatility regimes in short-term interest rate changes are associated with high volatility in yields of all maturities and higher covariances (Table 5-5) .

**TABLE 5–4**
*Correlations of Interest Rate Changes by Maturity*
*U.S. Treasury Securities (Period 1/5/62–11/26/93)*

|  | 3 Mo | 6 Mo | 1 Yr | 3 Yr | 5 Yr | 10 Yr |
|---|---|---|---|---|---|---|
| *All* |  | N = 1,664 |  |  |  |  |
| 3 mo | 1.00 |  |  |  |  |  |
| 6 mo | 0.92 | 1.00 |  |  |  |  |
| 1 yr | 0.65 | 0.73 | 1.00 |  |  |  |
| 3 yr | 0.57 | 0.66 | 0.92 | 1.00 |  |  |
| 5 yr | 0.51 | 0.61 | 0.87 | 0.95 | 1.00 |  |
| 10 yr | 0.47 | 0.56 | 0.81 | 0.91 | 0.93 | 1.00 |
| *Expansion* |  | N = 1,395 |  |  |  |  |
| 3 mo | 1.00 |  |  |  |  |  |
| 6 mo | 0.92 | 1.00 |  |  |  |  |
| 1 yr | 0.59 | 0.68 | 1.00 |  |  |  |
| 3 yr | 0.52 | 0.62 | 0.91 | 1.00 |  |  |
| 5 yr | 0.45 | 0.55 | 0.84 | 0.93 | 1.00 |  |
| 10 yr | 0.44 | 0.53 | 0.79 | 0.90 | 0.91 | 1.00 |
| *Recession* |  | N = 269 |  |  |  |  |
| 3 mo | 1.00 |  |  |  |  |  |
| 6 mo | 0.92 | 1.00 |  |  |  |  |
| 1 yr | 0.70 | 0.79 | 1.00 |  |  |  |
| 3 yr | 0.62 | 0.71 | 0.94 | 1.00 |  |  |
| 5 yr | 0.59 | 0.68 | 0.91 | 0.97 | 1.00 |  |
| 10 yr | 0.51 | 0.60 | 0.84 | 0.92 | 0.95 | 1.00 |
| *Low Variance* |  | N = 1,365 |  |  |  |  |
| 3 mo | 1.00 |  |  |  |  |  |
| 6 mo | 0.86 | 1.00 |  |  |  |  |
| 1 yr | 0.54 | 0.67 | 1.00 |  |  |  |
| 3 yr | 0.46 | 0.59 | 0.90 | 1.00 |  |  |
| 5 yr | 0.41 | 0.52 | 0.80 | 0.91 | 1.00 |  |
| 10 yr | 0.37 | 0.48 | 0.75 | 0.88 | 0.89 | 1.00 |
| *High Variance* |  | N = 299 |  |  |  |  |
| 3 mo | 1.00 |  |  |  |  |  |
| 6 mo | 0.94 | 1.00 |  |  |  |  |
| 1 yr | 0.68 | 0.76 | 1.00 |  |  |  |
| 3 yr | 0.63 | 0.71 | 0.94 | 1.00 |  |  |
| 5 yr | 0.59 | 0.67 | 0.91 | 0.97 | 1.00 |  |
| 10 yr | 0.55 | 0.63 | 0.86 | 0.93 | 0.96 | 1.00 |

Source: Federal Reserve, H15 Releases and database for various years.

**TABLE 5–5**
*Correlations of Interest Changes by Maturity*
*High-Volatility Regimes (10/5/79–1/7/83)*

|        | 3 Mo | 6 Mo | 1 Yr | 3 Yr | 5 Yr | 10 Yr |
|--------|------|------|------|------|------|-------|
| All    |      | N = 170 |   |      |      |       |
| 3 mo   | 1.00 |      |      |      |      |       |
| 6 mo   | 0.94 | 1.00 |      |      |      |       |
| 1 yr   | 0.68 | 0.75 | 1.00 |      |      |       |
| 3 yr   | 0.63 | 0.71 | 0.95 | 1.00 |      |       |
| 5 yr   | 0.58 | 0.67 | 0.92 | 0.97 | 1.00 |       |
| 10 yr  | 0.55 | 0.63 | 0.88 | 0.94 | 0.97 | 1.00  |

Source: Federal Reserve, H15 Releases and database for various years.

2. During high-volatility regimes, yield curves may be considerably different from those in periods of low volatility.

3. Changes in interest rate volatility regimes are not predictable, so that changes in interest rate sensitivity are also not predictable.

The parallel shift assumption of the agencies' proposal is clearly not supported by the evidence. Even more important, the stochastic model, incorporating conclusions based on historical data, gives a different interpretation to interest rate changes. For example, during periods of recession, interest rates tend to fall, but tend to be more volatile than when the economy is expanding and they are rising. For static models, including that of the agencies, the fall in interest rates suggests rising bank equity values. However, increased interest rate volatility means that interest rate levels and rate relationships among different maturities have become less predictable. The result is that the reliability of estimates of the changes in bank equity values declines and interest rate risk increases. In contrast, during periods of expansion, with rising interest rates, volatility tends to be low. Interest rates are more predictable. The result is greater reliability for expected changes in economic value—that is, less interest rate risk, *ceteris paribus*.

## CONCLUSIONS

The agencies' approach to measuring and evaluating interest rate risk reflects a static model, based on the concept of duration with a convexity correction. Exposure is determined by shocking the model with a ±200 bp increase in all interest rates—a parallel shift of the yield curve. However, the index of exposure (IRR index), as the agencies have constructed it, behaves perversely with increases in equity and reductions in leverage.

Other static measures, based on proportional changes in equity rather than the ratio of equity to bank assets, would be preferable. However, a more fundamental criticism of the agencies' model is that it does not account for the relationships between interest rate risk, interest rate volatility, and twists of the yield curve. Understanding the nature of interest rate volatility, as shown in this chapter, is critical to understanding the consequences of interest rate risk for bank soundness. It is also critical in understanding shifts and twists of the yield curve which have independent effects on the market value of equity. It would be possible, nevertheless, to incorporate yield curve twists in a static model; critical twists associated with particular portfolios could be identified on a bank-by-bank basis.

The static approach, nevertheless, remains deficient because it ignores the dynamics of interest rate and term structure changes. In this chapter we have introduced a dynamic and stochastic model that would remedy these deficiencies. It reveals how changes in the market value of bank equity are directly related to interest rate volatility and dependent on the correlation of interest rates of different maturities. In this context, there is empirical evidence that interest rate volatility and twists of the yield curve are related, and that both can have a major impact on bank exposure.

In Chapter 6, the issue of capital adequacy with regard to interest rate risk is considered. We propose a different approach, based on the analysis of this chapter, that directly employs dynamic and stochastic changes in interest rates and develops a more realistic method for determining needed capital.

## Appendix A

The model presented in equation (1) of the text is elaborated to develop a total elasticity measure of equity value changes with respect to interest rate changes. Similar to an arc elasticity, it indicates the effect of a change in the opportunity cost of equity $(1 + y_j)$ on equity value. Using equation (2) and recalling that the product of $\lambda_j$ and $dy$ is the total proportional change in the economic value of assets or liabilities with $dy$ assumed the same for each, elasticities may be calculated as follows:

$$\xi_A = \lambda_A \, dy \left( \frac{(1 + y_A)}{dy} \right) = \lambda_A (1 + y_A)$$

$$\xi_L = \lambda_L \, dy \left( \frac{(1 + y_L)}{dy} \right) = \lambda_L (1 + y_L)$$

(A–1)

Substituting for $\lambda_j$ into equation (2) for the change in the economic value of equity and collecting terms:

$$\frac{dE}{A} = \left[ \frac{(1 + y_L)\xi_A - (1 + y_A)\xi_L}{(1 + y_L)(1 + y_A)} \frac{L}{A} \right] dy$$

(A–2)

## Appendix B
### The Change in Economic Value of Equity in Terms of Asset and Liability Changes

The agencies' proposal presents the change in the economic value of bank equity resulting from a change in interest rates as a proportion of the economic value of bank assets. It expresses this as the sum of interest rate risk weights for each asset, liability, and off–balance sheet item times the amount of each item divided by total assets. Conceptually, this model accounts for interest rate changes as they affect assets and liabilities (ignoring off–balance sheet items for simplicity) as a duration of assets and liabilities adjusted for the convexity in the value–interest rate relationship for each portfolio item. This is essentially a Taylor series expansion of each item with regard to a constant change in interest rates (as assumed by the parallel shift of the yield articulated in the agencies' proposal).

Defining the change in equity as the change in assets less the change in liabilities:

$$dE \equiv dA - dL = \sum_i^m dA_i - \sum_j^l dL_j$$

(B–1)

Using a Taylor expansion to approximate the change in each of the asset and liability elements with respect to a common change in interest rate and truncating all powers greater than the powers of 2:

$$\frac{dA_i}{A_i} = \left[\frac{\partial A_i}{\partial y_i}\frac{dy_i}{A_i}A_i + \frac{1}{2}\frac{\partial^2 A_i}{\partial y_i^2}\frac{dy_i^2}{A_i}A_i\right]$$

$$\frac{dL_j}{L_j} = \left[\frac{\partial L_j}{\partial y_j}\frac{dy_j}{A_j}L_j + \frac{1}{2}\frac{\partial^2 L_j}{\partial y_j^2}\frac{dy_j^2}{L_j}L_j\right]$$

(B–2)

The terms $dA_i/A_i$ and $dL_j/L_j$ are analogous (continuous equivalent) to the risk weights for each element as the proportional change in the economic value of the element with respect to the interest rate change (Tables 5–6 and 5–7). Risk-weight derivations are in Table 5-8. The equivalent of the net risk weighted position to assets ratio, equation (4) in the text, is found by substituting equations (B–2) into equation (B–1) and dividing through by total assets, $A$:

$$\frac{dE}{A} = \frac{1}{A}\sum_i^m\left[\frac{\partial A_i}{\partial y_i}\frac{dy_i}{A_i}A_i + \frac{1}{2}\frac{\partial^2 A_i}{\partial y_i^2}\frac{dy_i^2}{A_i}A_i\right]$$

$$- \frac{L}{A}\sum_j^l\left[\frac{\partial L_j}{\partial y_j}\frac{dy_j}{L_j}L_j + \frac{1}{2}\frac{\partial^2 L_j}{\partial y_j^2}\frac{dy_j^2}{L_j}L_j\right]\frac{1}{L}$$

(B–3)

Essentially, this relationship is the proportional change in assets less the leverage weight of the proportional change in liabilities due to interest rate changes—the agencies' interest rate risk exposure measure.

## Bank Equity Value and Modeling Changes in Interest Rates as Stochastic Processes

Using this general model presented in equations (1) and (2) in the text, the approach used in this appendix is to relate changes in bank equity value to the interest rate sensitivity of bank assets and liabilities. As in the above simple model of the changes in bank equity, the value of equity ($E$) of a bank is defined as the market value of assets ($A$) less the market value of liabilities ($L$), and assets are composed of separate investments (e.g., real property, loans) and liabilities are, likewise, composed of separate liability issues (e.g., CDs, subordinated debt, transactions accounts, etc.). The yield to maturity of each of these asset and liability elements may be different and representing a different maturity. The interest sensitivity of each of these may also be different, reflecting the terms of the asset or liability contract. Thus, each element is likely to

**TABLE 5–6**
*Interest Rate Risk Worksheet (200 Basis Point Rising Rate Scenario)*
*(Reporting Institution: Sample Bank, Date: 12/31/92)*

|  | Total | Risk Risk Weights | Total Risk-Weighted Positions | Weighted Positions |
|---|---|---|---|---|
| I. Interest-sensitive assets |  |  |  |  |
| 1. ARMs, FRMs, asset-backed securities, consumer loans |  |  | (A) × (B) |  |
| a. Up to 3 months | $5,500 | −0.10% | $6 |  |
| b. 3 to 12 months | 4,950 | −0.50 | 25 |  |
| c. 1 to 3 years | 4,050 | −1.60 | 65 |  |
| d. 3 to 5 years | 4,166 | −3.00 | 125 |  |
| e. 5 to 10 years | 6,620 | −5.30 | 351 |  |
| f. 10 to 20 years | 6,454 | −8.80 | 368 |  |
| g. Greater than 20 years | 10,430 | −9.20 | 960 |  |
| 2. Zero- or low-coupon securities |  |  |  |  |
| a. Up to 3 months | $1,000 | −0.25% | ($3) |  |
| b. 3 to 12 months | 1,000 | −1.20 | (12) |  |
| c. 1 to 3 years | 1,000 | −3.70 | (37) |  |
| d. 3 to 5 years | 0 | −7.40 | 0 |  |
| e. 5 to 10 years | 0 | −13.30 | 0 |  |
| f. 10 to 20 years | 0 | −24.90 | 0 |  |
| g. Greater than 20 years | 0 | −38.00 | 0 |  |
| 3. "All other" securities, loans, and trading accounts |  |  |  |  |
| a. Up to 3 months | $26,672 | −0.25% | ($67) |  |
| b. 3 to 12 months | 28,432 | −1.20 | (341) |  |
| c. 1 to 3 years | 31,136 | −3.50 | (1,090) |  |
| d. 3 to 5 years | 19,728 | −6.40 | (1,263) |  |
| e. 5 to 10 years | 10,564 | −10.20 | (1,078) |  |
| f. 10 to 20 years | 8,837 | −14.90 | (1,317) |  |
| g. Greater than 20 years | 9,462 | −17.60 | (1,665) |  |
| 4. High-risk mortgage securities |  |  |  |  |
| a. Self-reporting | $2,000 |  | $160 |  |
| b. Risk-weighing | 1,000 | −38.00% | (380) |  |
| 5.Total interest-sensitive assets | $183,000 |  | ($9,190) | ($9,190) |
| II. All other assets | $3,000 |  |  |  |
| III. Total assets | $186,000 |  |  |  |

*continued*

**TABLE 5–6—*continued***
*Interest Rate Risk Worksheet (200 Basis Point Rising Rate Scenario)*
*(Reporting Institution: Sample Bank, Date: 12/31/92)*

| | Total | Risk Weights | Risk-Weighted Positions | Total Risk-Weighted Positions |
|---|---|---|---|---|
| IV. Interest-sensitive liabilities | | | | |
|   1. Non-maturity deposits, time deposits, and "all other" | | | | |
|     a. Up to 3 months | $23,083 | 0.25% | $58 | |
|     b. 3 to 12 months | 74,582 | 1.20 | 895 | |
|     c. 1 to 3 years | 51,321 | 3.70 | 1,899 | |
|     d. 3 to 5 years | 17,090 | 6.90 | 1,179 | |
|     e. 5 to 10 years | 64 | 11.60 | 7 | |
|     f. 10 to 20 years | 0 | 18.70 | 0 | |
|     g. Greater than 20 years | 0 | 24.00 | 0 | |
|   2. Total interest-sensitive liabilities | $166,140 | | $4,038 | |
| V. Non–interest-sensitive liabilities | $860 | | | |
| VI. Total liabilities | $167,000 | | $4,038 | $4,038 |
| VII. Equity capital | $19,001 | | | |
| VIII. Off–balance sheet positions | | | | |
|   1. Interest rate contracts | | | | |
|     a. Up to 3 months | $4,000 | –0.25% | ($10) | |
|     b. 3 to 12 months | 500 | –1.20 | ($6) | |
|     c. 1 to 3 years | (4,050) | –3.50 | $142 | |
|     d. 3 to 5 years | (450) | –6.40 | $29 | |
|     e. 5 to 10 years | 0 | –10.20 | $0 | |
|     f. 10 to 20 years | 0 | –14.90 | $0 | |
|     g. Greater than 20 years | 0 | –17.60 | $0 | |
|   2. Mortgage and other amortizing contracts | | | | |
|     a. Up to 3 months | $1,000 | –0.10% | ($1) | |
|     b. 3 to 12 months | 0 | –0.50 | 0 | |
|     c. 1 to 3 years | (1,000) | –1.60 | 16 | |
|     d. 3 to 5 years | 0 | –3.00 | 0 | |
|     e. 5 to 10 years | 0 | –5.30 | 0 | |
|     f. 10 to 20 years | 0 | –8.80 | 0 | |
|     g. Greater than 20 years | 0 | –9.20 | 0 | |
|   3. Total off–balance sheet positions | $0 | | $170 | $170 |
| Net risk-weighted position | | | | ($4,981.86) |
| Net position/assets | | | | –2.68% |

**TABLE 5–7**
*Interest Rate Risk Worksheet (200 Basis Point Declining Rate Scenario)*
*(Reporting Institution: Sample Bank, Date: 12/31/92)*

|  | Total | Risk Weights | Risk-Weighted Positions | Total Risk-Weighted Positions |
|---|---|---|---|---|
| I. Interest-sensitive assets | | | | |
| 1. ARMs, FRMs, asset-backed securities, consumer loans | | | (A) × (B) | |
| a. Up to 3 months | $5,500 | 0.10% | $6 | |
| b. 3 to 12 months | 4,950 | 0.60 | 20 | |
| c. 1 to 3 years | 4,050 | 1.70 | 69 | |
| d. 3 to 5 years | 4,166 | 3.10 | 129 | |
| e. 5 to 10 years | 6,620 | 3.40 | 225 | |
| f. 10 to 20 years | 6,454 | 5.90 | 381 | |
| g. Greater than 20 years | 10,430 | 3.60 | 375 | |
| 2. Zero- or low-coupon securities | | | | |
| a. Up to 3 months | $1,000 | 0.25% | $3 | |
| b. 3 to 12 months | 1,000 | 1.20 | 12 | |
| c. 1 to 3 years | 1,000 | 3.90 | 39 | |
| d. 3 to 5 years | 0 | 8.00 | 0 | |
| e. 5 to 10 years | 0 | 15.60 | 0 | |
| f. 10 to 20 years | 0 | 33.50 | 0 | |
| g. Greater than 20 years | 0 | 61.90 | 0 | |
| 3. "All other" securities, loans, and trading account | | | | |
| a. Up to 3 months | $26,672 | 0.25% | $67 | |
| b. 3 to 12 months | 28,432 | 1.20 | 341 | |
| c. 1 to 3 years | 31,136 | 3.70 | 1,152 | |
| d. 3 to 5 years | 19,728 | 7.00 | 1,381 | |
| e. 5 to 10 years | 10,564 | 11.70 | 1,236 | |
| f. 10 to 20 years | 8,837 | 19.00 | 1,679 | |
| g. Greater than 20 years | 9,462 | 24.60 | 2,328 | |
| 4. High-risk mortgage securities | | | | |
| a. Self-reporting | $2,000 | | ($200) | |
| b. Risk-weighing | 1,000 | −38.00% | (380) | |
| 5. Total interest-sensitive assets | $183,000 | | $8,871 | $8,871 |
| II. All other assets | $3,000 | | | |
| III. Total assets | $186,000 | | | |

*continued*

**TABLE 5–7—***continued*
*Interest Rate Risk Worksheet (200 Basis Point Declining Rate Scenario)*
*(Reporting Institution: Sample Bank, Date: 12/31/92)*

| | Total | Risk Weights | Risk-Weighted Positions | Total Risk-Weighted Positions |
|---|---|---|---|---|
| IV. Interest-sensitive liabilities | | | | |
| 1. Non-maturity deposits, time deposits, and " all other" | | | | |
| a. Up to 3 months | $38,583 | –0.25% | ($96) | |
| b. 3 to 12 months | 77.582 | –1.20 | (931) | |
| c. 1 to 3 years | 39,821 | –3.90 | (1,553) | |
| d. 3 to 5 years | 10,090 | –7.50 | (757) | |
| e. 5 to 10 years | 64 | –13.50 | (9) | |
| f. 10 to 20 years | 0 | –24.50 | 0 | |
| g. Greater than 20 years | 0 | –36.00 | 0 | |
| 2. Total interest-sensitive liabilities | $166,140 | | ($3,346) | |
| V. Non–interest-sensitive liabilities | $860 | | | |
| VI. Total liabilities | $167,000 | | ($3,346) | ($3,346) |
| VII. Equity capital | $19,001 | | | |
| VIII. Off–balance sheet positions | | | | |
| 1. Interest rate contracts | | | | |
| a. Up to 3 months | $4,000 | 0.25% | $10 | |
| b. 3 to 12 months | 500 | 1.20 | 6 | |
| c. 1 to 3 years | (4,050) | 3.70 | (150) | |
| d. 3 to 5 years | (450) | 7.00 | (32) | |
| e. 5 to 10 years | 0 | 11.70 | 0 | |
| f. 10 to 20 years | 0 | 19.00 | 0 | |
| g. Greater than 20 years | 0 | 24.60 | 0 | |
| 2. Mortgage and other amortizing contracts | | | | |
| a. Up to 3 months | $1,000 | 0.10% | $1 | |
| b. 3 to 12 months | 0 | 0.60 | 0 | |
| c. 1 to 3 years | (1,000) | 1.70 | (17) | |
| d. 3 to 5 years | 0 | 3.10 | 0 | |
| e. 5 to 10 years | 0 | 3.40 | 0 | |
| f. 10 to 20 years | 0 | 5.90 | 0 | |
| g. Greater than 20 years | 0 | 3.60 | 0 | |
| 3. Total off–balance sheet positions | $0 | | ($181) | ($181) |
| Net risk-weighted position | | | | $5,344.31 |
| Net position/assets | | | | 2.87% |

# TABLE 5-8
## Derivation of Risk Weights

| Time band | Maturity | Coupon | Initial Price (% of Par) | Initial PSA/ABS[e] | Scenario 1: 200 Basis Point Rise | | | Scenario 2: 200 Basis Point Decline | | |
|---|---|---|---|---|---|---|---|---|---|---|
| | | | | | Expected PSA/ABS | Price (% of Par) | % Change in Present Value (Risk Weights) | Expected PSA/ABS | Price (% of Par) | % Change in Present Value (Risk Weights) |
| *Amortizing instruments* | | | | | | | | | | |
| 0–3 months | 1.5 months | 8.5% | 100.00% | 1.0% ABS | 1.0% ABS | 99.90% | -0.10% | 1.0% ABS | 100.10% | 0.10% |
| 3–12 months | 7.5 months | 8.5 | 100.00 | 1.0 ABS | 1.0 ABS | 99.50 | -0.50 | 1.0 ABS | 100.60 | 0.60 |
| 1–3 years | 2 years | 8.5 | 100.00 | 1.0 ABS | 1.0 ABS | 98.40 | -1.60 | 1.0 ABS | 101.70 | 1.70 |
| 3–5 years | 4 years | 8.5 | 100.00 | 1.0 ABS | 1.0 ABS | 97.00 | -3.00 | 1.0 ABS | 103.10 | 3.10 |
| 5–10 years | 7.5 years | 7.0[a] | 100.00 | 166 PSA[c] | 137 PSA[c] | 94.70 | -5.30 | 501 PSA[c] | 103.40 | 3.40 |
| 10–20 years | 15 years | 7.0%[a] | 100.00 | 166 PSA[c] | 137 PSA[c] | 91.20 | -8.80 | 501 PSA[c] | 105.90 | 5.90 |
| Over 20 years | 25 years | 7.5[b] | 100.00 | 242 PSA[c] | 146 PSA[c] | 90.80 | -9.20 | 590 PSA[c] | 103.60 | 3.60 |
| *All other instruments* | | | | | | | | | | |
| 0–3 months | 1.5 months | 8.5% | 100.00%[d] | | | 99.75% | -0.25% | | 100.25% | 0.25% |
| 3–12 months | 7.5 months | 8.5 | 100.00[d] | | | 98.80 | -1.20 | | 101.20 | 1.20 |
| 1–3 years | 2 years | 8.5 | 100.00 | | | 96.50 | -3.50 | | 103.70 | 3.70 |
| 3–5 years | 4 years | 8.5 | 100.00 | | | 93.60 | -6.40 | | 107.00 | 7.00 |
| 5–10 years | 7.5 years | 8.5 | 100.00 | | | 89.80 | -10.20 | | 111.70 | 11.70 |
| 10–20 years | 15 years | 8.5 | 100.00 | | | 85.10[a] | -14.90 | | 119.00 | 19.00 |
| Over 20 years | 25 years | 8.5 | 100.00 | | | 82.40 | -17.60 | | 124.60 | 24.60 |
| *Liabilities* | | | | | | | | | | |
| 0–3 months | 1.5 months | 4.75% | 100.00%[d] | | | 99.75% | 0.25% | | 100.25% | -0.25% |
| 3–12 months | 7.5 months | 4.75 | 100.00[d] | | | 98.80 | 1.20 | | 101.20 | -1.20 |
| 1–3 years | 2 years | 4.75 | 100.00 | | | 96.30 | 3.70 | | 103.90 | -3.90 |
| 3–5 years | 4 years | 4.75 | 100.00 | | | 93.10 | 6.90 | | 107.50 | -7.50 |
| 5–10 years | 7.5 years | 4.75 | 100.00 | | | 88.40 | 11.60 | | 113.50 | -13.50 |
| 10–20 years | 15 years | 4.75 | 100.00 | | | 81.30 | 18.70 | | 124.50 | -24.50 |
| Over 20 years | 25 years | 4.75 | 100.00 | | | 76.00 | 24.00 | | 136.00 | -36.00 |
| *Zero- or low-coupon securities* | | | | | | | | | | |
| 0–3 months | 1.5 months | 8.5% | 98.97% | | | 98.72% | -0.25% | | 99.22% | 0.25% |
| 3–12 months | 7.5 months | 8.5 | 94.95 | | | 93.81 | -1.20 | | 96.09 | 1.20 |
| 1–3 years | 2 years | 8.5 | 84.66 | | | 81.53 | -3.70 | | 87.96 | 3.90 |
| 3–5 years | 4 years | 8.5 | 71.68 | | | 66.38 | -7.40 | | 77.41 | 8.00 |
| 5–10 years | 7.5 years | 8.5 | 53.56 | | | 46.44 | -13.30 | | 61.92 | 15.60 |
| 10–20 years | 15 years | 8.5 | 28.69 | | | 21.55 | -24.90 | | 38.30 | 33.50 |
| Over 20 years | 25 years | 8.5 | 12.48 | | | 7.74 | -38.00 | | 20.21 | 61.90 |

[a] Current coupon of 15-year conventional mortgage securities as of 12/31/92.
[b] Current coupon of 30-year conventional mortgage securities as of 12/31/92.
[c] Consensus of dealer prepayment estimates for 15- and 30-year conventional mortgage securities for scenarios as of 12/31/92.
[d] Actual initial price is slightly less than par.
[e] PSA: Assumed prepayment schedule adjustments from each specified interest rate change based on normal prepayment adjustments of mortgages of each maturity.

have associated with it a unique duration and convexity as well as a different market value trend over time (e.g., a zero-coupon bond will increase in market value as time to maturity decreases).

We can define a stochastic process for interest rates as an Ito process of the form:

$$dy_i = f(t, y_i) \, dt + \sigma(t, y_i) \, dz(t) \qquad \text{(B–4)}$$

where $z(t)$ is a Wiener process with zero mean and unit variance and $\sigma(t, y_i)$ is the standard deviation of $dy_i$.[17]

The function $f(t, y_i)$ is a drift function for interest rates, either positive or negative, or a function exhibiting mean reversion and dependent upon $y_i$ and time ($t$). For interest rates, we hypothesize that this function is zero, so that the expected change in a yield to maturity, for any term, is zero. This hypothesis is supported by a number of studies of the term structure of interest rates[18] and theoretical considerations of the behavior of interest rate futures contracts.[19] The yield to maturity for each asset and liability in the portfolio will be assumed to follow this diffusion process with a variance associated with the particular asset or liability.

$$dy_i = \sigma(t, y_i) \, dz(t) \qquad \text{(B–5)}$$

The change in the market value of equity is a function of the interest rates of each of the assets and liabilities and can be stated in terms of each of these interest rate processes by employing Ito's lemma.[20] In general, the change in the market value of equity is (assets have positive signs and liabilities have negative signs):

$$dE(Y, t) = \sum_i \frac{\partial E}{\partial y_i} \, dy_i + \frac{\partial E}{\partial t} \, dt + \frac{1}{2} \sum_i \sum_j \sigma_{ij} \frac{\partial^2 E}{\partial y_i \, \partial y_j} \, dt \qquad \text{(B–6)}$$

where $Y$ is the vector of interest rates, the elements of which are the yields to maturity of the assets and liabilities in the portfolio, and $\sigma_{ij}$ is the covariance of interest rate changes between interest rates on assets and liabilities ($\sigma_{ii}$ is the variance). Upon substitution of equation (B–5) into (B–6), the diffusion process for equity can be expressed in terms of the process for interest rates:

$$dE(Y, t) = \sum_i \frac{\partial E}{\partial y_i} \, \sigma_i(y_i, t) \, dz + \frac{\partial E}{\partial t} \, dt + \frac{1}{2} \sum_i \sum_j \sigma_{ij} \frac{\partial^2 E}{\partial y_i \, \partial y_j} \, dt \qquad \text{(B–7)}$$

By definition, $\sigma_{ij}$ can be expressed in terms of the correlation coefficient of interest rate changes, $\rho_{ij}$, and the standard deviation of yield change $i$ and $j$:

$$\sigma_{ij} = \rho_{ij}\sigma_i\sigma_j \tag{B-8}$$

From expression (B–7), it is clear that changes in equity value with respect to changes in interest rates require specification of the standard deviation (volatility) of each asset and liability interest rate and the correlation among interest rates changes.

The partial change in equity value with respect to a partial change in an interest rate—the first set of terms in equation (B–7)—is equal to the change in the price of the asset or liability with respect to its yield to maturity times the number of units. This can be written as:

$$\frac{\partial E}{\partial y_i} = n_i \frac{\partial P_i}{\partial y_i} \tag{B-9}$$

where $n_i$ is the number of units of element $i$ and $\partial P_i/\partial y_i$ is the partial derivative of the price of element $i$ with respect to its yield to maturity. Multiplying and dividing each asset and liability by its respective price $P_i$, and the interest rate factor $(1 + y_i)$, the result is, in terms of the right-hand side of equation (B–9):

$$n_i \frac{\partial P_i}{\partial y_i} \frac{(1 + y_i)}{P_i} \frac{P_i}{(1 + y_i)} = n_i D_i \frac{P_i}{(1 + y_i)} \tag{B-10}$$

where $D_i$ is Macaulay's duration and $n_i P_i$ is the value of the amount of asset or liability $i$. Multiplying and dividing each element by total assets $A$, equation (B–10) can be transformed into the share of assets of each element, $w_i = n_i P_i/A$, duration, and the interest rate factor:

$$n_i D_i \frac{P_i}{(1 + y_i)} \frac{A}{A} = w_i D_i \frac{A}{(1 + y_i)} \tag{B-11}$$

Using equation (B–11) and dividing equation (B–7) through by $E$, the change in $E$ can be expressed as a proportional change in the value of equity due to changes in the yields to maturity of assets and liabilities and how they behave over time:

$$\frac{dE(Y, t)}{E} = \frac{A}{E} \sum_i \frac{w_i D_i}{(1 + y_i)} \sigma_i (y_i, t) \, dz + \frac{\partial E}{\partial t} \frac{dt}{E} + \frac{1}{2} \sum_i \sum_j \sigma_{ij} \frac{\partial^2 E}{\partial y_i \partial y_j} \frac{dt}{E} \tag{B-12}$$

The partial derivative of $E$ with respect to time, $\partial E/\partial t$, can be restated in terms of the partial derivatives of components of assets and liabilities with respect to time. These terms show the movement of the values of assets and liabilities through time and reflect the market value of these elements as they reach maturity. For example, the price of a U.S. Government bond with fixed coupons and a repayment of principal at maturity will move toward the par value of the bond. If the bond is presently selling at a discount, the price will rise toward the par value, while if it is selling at a premium, it will decline to the par value, *ceteris paribus*.

The final term in equation (B–12) represents the changes in the slope of equity value with respect to interest rate changes due to changes in interest rates. This term measures the convexity of the economic value of equity with respect to each of the interest rates of assets and liabilities in the bank's portfolio. These partial second derivatives can be restated in terms of each of the asset and liability elements in the bank's portfolio using equation (B–9). It is important to realize that the value of equity changes will be significantly affected by the correlation among interest rates of different assets and liabilities *and* the convexity of each of these elements. To the extent that the correlation and the variance of each interest rate are constant over time, these values can be treated as parameters in the simulations and historical data can be used to estimate these values. However, if they are time-varying, they become subject to forecast just as are levels of interest rates. The evidence (see Hanweck and Hanweck, 1993, and Figure 5–2) suggests that interest rate volatility is time-varying and covariances will vary depending on the volatility of interest rates.

## NOTES

1. A principal deficiency of risk-based capital requirements is that they are rooted in book value. The final rules adopted by the agencies for prompt corrective action can be found in the Federal Reserve Board press release of September 18, 1992.

2. The model developed by the banking agencies is made explicit in Houpt and Embersit (1991).

3. This is accomplished by solving equation 9(a) in Chapter 4 for $dE/A$ [noting that $dE/A$ is $dA/A + (dL/L)(L/A)$].

4. Normally for bank asset and liability portfolios, where convexity-adjusted durations are negative, the relationship between the relative changes in assets and liabilities is such that $\lambda_A < \lambda_L < 0$.

5. This ratio is negative, as noted, because the risk-weighted position of assets is negative and exceeds, in absolute value, the positive risk-weighted positions of liabilities and off–balance sheet items. The ratio of the net risk-weighted position to assets is found on the last line of Table 5–6.

6.  As noted in the text, the algebraic reason for the increase in the IRR index with an increase in capital is simply that the difference between risk-weighted assets and risk-weighted liabilities (the net risk-weighted position) increases as risk-weighted liabilities get less weight as leverage is reduced. It should be noted that it is only on the basis of some restrictive assumptions that the IRR index rises asymptotically toward the IRR index of assets when capital is added. It was assumed that the risk weights of individual liabilities and assets, and the value of assets, are constant.

7.  This perverse behavior in the IRR index has been recognized in the agencies' July 1992 proposal ("Comment 10," pp. 46–47). But its significance has been minimized as "correctable" through a minor adjustment. The agencies suggested normalizing each bank's risk-weighted liabilities by the product of the bank's ratio of assets to liabilities $(A/L)$ and the industry average ratio of liabilities to assets $(s)$. The result of this operation is to make the adjusted IRR index equal to $D_A - D_L \times s$, where $D_A$ and $D_L$ are durations of assets and liabilities, and independent of changes in leverage with asset and liability durations constant. As the agencies recognize, this adjustment assigns the same risk measure to banks with the same durations of assets and liabilities, but not the same duration of equity. The absence of reaction of the adjusted index to greater equity is no more acceptable than is an increasing unadjusted index and does not remedy the defect. The problem remains uncorrected in the most recent proposal.

8.  The use of swaps, futures, and options is particularly important as banks invest more heavily in mortgages and mortgage-backed securities where cash flows have complex relationships with market interest rates and the presence of an embedded option makes them subject to the volatility of interest rate changes in complex ways. Certain hedging instruments, such as swaps, used to offset interest rate risk may at the same time increase credit risk. In such cases, conventional risk-adjusted capital standards may substitute for incremental capital requirements associated with interest rate risk.

9.  This model is similar to the duration model developed in Hanweck and Shull (1993) in commenting on the agencies' July 1993 proposal.

10. On these points, see Cox, Ingersoll, and Ross (1985); Fisher and Weil (1971), Bierwag, Kaufman, and Toevs (1982); and Fabozzi (1993).

11. In a recent study, Cohen (1993, pp. 23–31) analyzed the effects of historical interest rate changes on seemingly duration-matched portfolios after accounting for convexity. He found that the greatest losses to these hypothetical bank portfolios were derived from interest rate changes other than parallel shifts in the yield curve.

12. The 1993 proposal suggested using data for the period 1984 to the present and revising these estimates on a biennial frequency (Federal Reserve Release, September 14, 1993, pp. 22–29).

13. Hanweck and Hanweck (1993) provide a full discussion of this literature with respect to the time variance of the term premium of the short-term yield curve for 13-week and 26-week U.S. T-bills.

14. The probability of being in one of two regimes and the transition probability of moving from one regime to the other is computed using a Markov regime-switching model. The procedure used to estimate the parameters of the process follow the technique developed by Engle and Hamilton (1990), Hamilton (1990), and Cai (1992) and are explained in the Appendix to Hanweck and Hanweck (1993).

15. Hanweck and Hanweck (1993) use a Markov-ARCH regression to test various regime-switching hypotheses. They find that interest rate processes are substantially dominated by Markov regime switching rather than ARCH processes.

16. Periods of high volatility are those when the probability of being in a high-volatility regime exceeds 50 percent.

17. See Malliaris and Brock (1985, pp. 65–92) and Ingersoll (1987, Chapter 16).

18. See Hanweck and Hanweck (1993) for a review of the literature and evidence of a variable-term premium in the short-term yield curve.

19. This hypothesis follows if interest rates can be considered as having the martingale property of $E[y_{n+1} | y_1 \ldots y_n] = y_n$ (see Ingersoll, 1987, p. 403, for a similar hypothesis). See Samuelson (1965) for the establishment of futures prices in efficient markets as a martingale process.

20. See Malliaris and Brock (1985, pp. 80–89).

## REFERENCES

Bierwag, G. O., George G. Kaufman, and Alden L. Toevs. "Single Factor Duration Models in a Discrete General Equilibrium Framework," *Journal of Finance* 37 (May 1982), pp. 105–57.

Cai, Jun. "A Markov Model of Unconditional Variance in ARCH," Working Paper, Department of Finance, Kellogg Graduate School of Management, Northwestern University, November 1992.

Cohen, Hugh. "Beyond Duration: Measuring Interest Rate Exposure," *Economic Review* 78 (March–April, 1993), Federal Reserve Bank of Atlanta, pp. 23–31.

Cox, John C., Jonathan E. Ingersoll, Jr., and Stephen A. Ross. "A Theory of the Term Structure of Interest Rates," *Econometrica* 53 (1985), pp. 385–407.

Engle, Charles, and James D. Hamilton. "Long Swings in the Dollar: Are They in the Data and Do Markets Know It?" *American Economic Review* 80 (1990), pp. 869–713.

Fabozzi, Frank J. *Bond Markets: Analysis and Strategies.* 2nd ed. Englewood Cliffs, N.J.: Prentice Hall, 1993.

Federal Reserve Board, Press Release, *Interagency Advance Notice of Proposed Rulemaking to Revise Risk-Based Capital Standards,* July 30, 1992.

Federal Reserve Board, "Press Release on 'Prompt Corrective Action'," September 18, 1992.

Federal Reserve Board, Press Release, *Interagency Notice of Proposed Rulemaking to Revise Risk-Based Capital Standards,* September 14, 1993.

Fisher, Lawrence, and Roman L. Weil. "Coping with the Risk of Interest-Rate Fluctuations: Returns to Bondholders from Naive and Optimal Strategies," *Journal of Business* 44 (October 1971), pp. 408–31.

———— and ————. "Prudential Supervision to Manage Systematic Vulnerability," *Proceedings of a Conference on Bank Structure and Competition,* Federal Reserve Bank of Chicago, 1988, p. 602.

Hamilton, James D. "Analysis of Time Series Subject to Changes in Regime," *Journal of Econometrics* 45 (1990), pp. 39–70.

Hanweck, Gerald A., Sr., and Gerald A. Hanweck, Jr. "The Expectations Hypothesis of the Term Structure of Short-Term Interest Rates: Identifying the Presence of a Time-Varying Term Premium" (September 1993), presented at the Financial Management Association Meetings, Toronto, Canada, October 1993.

Hanweck, Gerald A., and Bernard Shull. "Interest Rate Risk and Capital Adequacy," *The Bankers Magazine* (September–October 1993), pp. 41–48.

Houpt, James, and James Embersit. "A Method for Evaluating Interest Rate Risk in U.S. Commercial Banks," *Federal Reserve Bulletin,* Board of Governors of the Federal Reserve System, August 1991.

Ingersoll, Jonathan E., Jr., *Theory of Financial Decision Making,* Bowman & Littlefield, Publishers Totowa, N.J., 1987.

Malliaris, A. G., and W. A. Brock. *Stochastic Methods In Economics and Finance.* Amsterdam: Elsevier Science Publishers, 1985.

Samuelson, Paul. "Proof that Properly Anticipated Prices Fluctuate Randomly," *Industrial Management Review,* Spring 1965, pp. 41–49.

## Chapter Six

# The Regulation of Interest Rate Risk: Practical Problems and Policy Issues

In Chapters 4 and 5, we described the several ways in which interest rate risk is measured and modeled. The models we reviewed included the "supervisory model" of the federal banking agencies and their proposed "minimum capital standard" approach to establish the amount of capital required to meet interest rate risk exposure.[1] The model and approach, which established a threshold for excess exposure and converted the excess into a credit risk equivalent, integrated interest rate risk and risk-based capital requirements in an explicit and precise way. However, it suffered from a number of important defects.

Here we review the agencies' 1995 proposal that reflects the as yet unfinished efforts of the federal agencies to accomplish the integration required by Congress. We also consider the nature of the problems the agencies appear to have encountered and the policy implications of the approach it appears they are likely to adopt. Finally, alternative approaches that might better serve both banks and the banking agencies are discussed.

## CONGRESSIONAL INTENT, THE 1993 PROPOSAL, AND THE 1995 "FINAL RULE"

Section 305 of the FDIC Improvement Act (FDICIA), passed on December 19, 1991, required the federal banking agencies to revise their "risk-based capital standards to take account of interest rate risk, among other types of risk."[2] It set a date of no later than

June 19, 1993 (18 months after the date the law was enacted), for publication of final regulations in the *Federal Register*. The federal banking agencies published a Notice of Proposed Rulemaking (NPR) on September 14, 1993, requesting comments by October 29, 1993.[3] The proposal outlined an exemption standard, a measurement system, a supervisory model, and two approaches for determining how much additional capital would be required—a minimum capital standards approach and a risk assessment approach.

The agencies' Final Rule was published in the *Federal Register* on August 2, 1995. It was accompanied by a proposed "Joint Agency Policy Statement" for "measuring and assessing bank interest rate risk exposure." As the banking agencies stated in issuing their Final Rule, they "have not met the . . . statutory date for publishing a final rule for this section of FDICIA."[4] In fact, the agencies overshot it by more than 2 years. Moreover, the "Final Rule" does not establish any formal system for incorporating interest rate risk into risk-based capital requirements; that is, it does not "codify a measurement framework for assessing the level of a bank's interest rate risk exposure" and does not establish a method for determining a capital charge for excess exposure.[5]

The Final Rule, according to the agencies' statement, implements the first step of a two-step process. It revises the "capital standards of the banking agencies to explicitly include a bank's exposure to declines in the economic value of its capital due to changes in interest rates as a factor that the banking agencies will consider in evaluating a bank's capital adequacy."[6] The policy statement is a proposal that details a measurement system for monitoring and assessing interest rate risk.[7]

Neither the Final Rule nor the policy statement establishes a capital charge for interest rate risk exposure. Rather, both reflect the agencies' adoption of a two-step process for implementing one. The Final Rule revises agencies' explicit standards. The policy statement describes a measurement system. Once the measurement system is finalized, the Final Rule and the policy statement will have constituted the first step.

Together, the two documents represent the adoption of what the agencies term the "risk assessment" approach for assessing a capital charge. The interest rate exposure revealed by the measurement system would constitute one "quantitative factor" to be used by examiners to evaluate a bank's capital position. Other quantitative factors would include a bank's historical performance, its earnings exposure to changes in interest rates. In addition, examiners will consider "qualitative" factors such as the adequacy of the bank's own interest rate risk management system.

At some later stage, the second step is contemplated. The agencies intend to establish an explicit minimum capital charge based on a bank's measured exposure, that is, to substitute a minimum capital standards approach. The agencies have reasoned that this step can be better accomplished after they have had some experience with the supervisory measurement and assessment process (the first step).[8]

The problems of regulating interest rate risk are manifest in the agencies' slow movement toward meeting congressional aims. It is worth reviewing key elements of the 1993 proposal to highlight these problems. A further discussion of why it has taken so long is undertaken the in Appendix to this chapter.

### Key Elements of the 1993 Proposal: Minimum Capital Standards

The agencies' Advance Notice of Proposed Rulemaking (ANPR) in August 1992 detailed a framework to measure the effect of a parallel shift in the yield curve on the value of a bank's equity. It included a supervisory model and a quantitative method for translating excess exposure into an explicit capital charge.

Roughly a year later, after substantial review, the agencies issued a Notice of Proposed Rulemaking (NPR; September 1993). The NPR was less rigid than the ANPR. It included an exemption from reporting requirements for low-risk banks.[9] The NPR equivocated on the use of the supervisory model to measure exposure to interest rate risk. A bank's own internal model might also be used. In either event, a parallel shift in the yield curve would serve to determine exposure.[10] It suggested that a minimum capital standards approach or a risk management approach might be adopted to determine the capital charge.

The supervisory model would require banks to report their assets, liabilities, and off–balance sheet positions in time bands (maturity buckets) based on remaining maturities or nearest repricing dates. A percentage change in the present value of a representative instrument for each time band, resulting from the hypothetical shift in the yield curve, would produce a risk weight for the financial instruments for each bank. Arithmetically, a bank's exposure would be the sum of the estimated changes in present value of its maturity bucket distributed positions.[11]

A predetermined threshold was to be set at a decline in the value of a bank's equity of 1.0 percent of total assets (for the 200 basis point shift in the yield curve). A greater decline would then be defined as an excess exposure. The capital charge would be determined by converting the dollar amount of excess exposure into an addition to risk-weighted assets which, in turn, would lower the bank's risk-based capital ratio. In effect, the excess exposure would be handled in about the same way as an addition to credit risk emanating, for example, from new loans to a real estate developer, farmer, or consumer. With each bank's exposure determined, the minimum capital standards approach then required that excess exposure be calculated and converted to a capital charge (see Tables 5-6 and 5-7 in Chapter 5).

An example provided by the agencies illustrated how the approach might work. Assume a bank with assets of $125 million, risk-weighted assets of $100 million, and capital of $10 million. Further assume that an evaluation of its interest rate risk, on the basis of the supervisory model, indicates an excess exposure of 0.8 percent, or $1 million; that is, it has an IRR index of 1.8 percent in absolute value. An addition to risk-adjusted assets, based on the $1 million exposure, would then reduce the bank's risk-based capital ratio. Any needed addition to capital would be derived from the minimum 8 percent risk-based capital ratio for "adequately capitalized banks," (Table 1–4 in Chapter 1) as defined by regulation under FDICIA.

Larger exposures would result in greater additions to risk-weighted assets and larger increments to capital to sustain any given risk-based ratio. A substantial exposure, without additions to capital, might lower the risk-based capital ratio so much as to move a bank to a lower capital adequacy level—for example, from "well capitalized" to "adequately capitalized." Excess exposure, not adequately offset by capital additions, might trigger prompt corrective action.[12] The risk assessment approach, on the other hand, would permit examiners to use the supervisory model among other sources of information to assess the level of interest rate risk. Measurement and evaluation—and, therefore, any capital charge—would be subject to examiner discretion.

## *Technical Problems Implicit in the 1993 Proposal*

Technical problems in the 1993 NPR are principally associated with the supervisory model and the minimum capital standards technique for translating interest rate risk into credit risk.[13] First, as indicated in Chapter 5, the interest rate risk index on which the 1993 minimum capital standards approach was based had severe limitations in determining capital adequacy. The agencies' index did not accurately measure the exposure of individual banks and, under reasonable assumptions, indicated more interest rate risk (and therefore a need for additional capital) as capital was added. Adding capital on the basis of certain threshold values of the index did not decrease interest rate risk as commonly measured by the duration, or by the elasticity of the value of a bank's equity value with respect to interest rate changes. Even substantial increases in capital would be limited in their measured effect.

More important, they might provide little decrease in the actual risk a bank confronted. For example, under either the risk assessment approach or the minimum capital standards approach, there appears to be no more than standard regulatory constraints on how any additional capital would be invested. Investments might lengthen or shorten asset maturities and durations—and thus alter the bank's interest rate risk and the IRR index—and even offset any interest rate risk reduction derived from additions to capital.

Finally, the 200 basis point, parallel shift scenario, from which subsequent calculations follow, is unrealistic.[14] There is a good deal of empirical evidence to indicate that interest rate volatility can shift erratically and that parallel shifts in the yield curve are, to say the least, unusual.

Underlying this willingness to find a parallel shift in the yield curve an acceptable simplification appears to be a belief that banks are at the greatest risk when interest rates are rising rapidly. This belief may reflect the influential impact of experience during the years between 1979 and 1982. We have examined historical changes in interest rates more systematically. These changes indicate that interest rate volatility and, therefore, the degree of bank exposure to interest rate risk are associated with distinct periods of time; that is, interest rate volatility is time-variant. High levels of exposure develop in periods of high interest rate volatility, that is, in high-volatility "regimes." Further, high-volatility regimes occur not when interest rates are rising, but when interest rates are falling.

Shifts in interest rate volatility regimes may be the single most important factor affecting bank exposure to interest rate risk. However, such shifts are not predictable. Therefore, the volatility of interest rates, their covariances among instruments of different maturity, and other relevant characteristics of interest rate changes that affect the level and changes in the shape of the yield curve are not predictable. This problem is not addressed in the agencies' proposal.

There is a need, then, to develop a more realistic framework within which interest rate scenarios might impair bank equity. The agencies' decision to further consider the matter before proceeding to a "second step" indicates as much.

## Policy Issues

There remain certain policy issues that the agencies do not seem to be considering at this time. In general, these relate to the question whether or not capital is an appropriate regulatory instrument for regulating interest rate risk. As noted in Chapter 3, the emergence of capital requirements as the regulatory instrument of choice is relatively recent, and there may be a temptation to extend them beyond their efficacy. Whether or not it makes sense to use capital requirements for purposes of regulating interest rate risk is discussed below along the following lines: (1) effectiveness in meeting regulatory and bank objectives, (2) effects on bank incentives, (3) relationship between interest rate risk and credit risk, and (4) practical problems in implementing a reasonable standard.

**1. Effectiveness.** In each of the models developed in Chapter 5, and most notably with respect to the supervisory model, there are limits to which increased capital requirements can effectively reduce a bank's interest rate risk exposure. In general, these limits are set by the duration of assets and convexity.

The existence of limits raises a question about the effectiveness of regulatory control. Can, in fact, the degree of restraint required always be established through incremental capital requirements? If so, to what extent will the agencies have to reduce bank leverage, and thereby raise bank costs, to establish the minimum protection they deem tolerable?

Further, as noted, empirical analysis indicates that interest rate risk exposure can shift abruptly and unpredictably. Bank capital, on the other hand, cannot be altered as quickly. This observation suggests that one should expect lags in the application of capital charges to meet interest rate risk—in both an upward and a downward direction. But capital charges have long-term effects on bank profitability. The net impact on bank profits over the long run is uncertain, but there is no reason to believe that it will be closely associated with the protection capital provides against interest rate risk. The question that emerges is whether requiring additional capital to control interest rate risk is the least expensive way for banks to deal with the problem. Are there lower-cost alternatives?

**2. Incentives.**   Risk-based capital requirements clearly introduce incentives to modify asset and liability management and, other things equal, lower the risk profiles of bank portfolios—for example, by encouraging a shift to government securities.[15] Integrating interest rate risk into risk-based capital requirements would seem to introduce similar incentives that would encourage banks to shorten the durations of assets and/or lengthen the durations of liabilities. In the agencies' 1993 proposal (Federal Reserve Board, 1993), banks that evidenced "low risk" by meeting certain conditions would be exempt from reporting. As noted, an estimate in the agencies' statement based on 1992 data indicated that about 8,400 banks with about 30 percent of bank assets would be exempt. A simple calculation, based on the rules for exemption indicates that banks having no more than about 16 percent of their total assets maturing in more than 5 years would be exempt.

The proposal established an incentive, then, for banks to reach for exempt status. While exempt status is not quite the "narrow bank," it certainly moves in that direction when coupled with credit risk weights that encourage the acquisition of government securities.

The question raised is just how significant these incentives will be in altering bank management choices—and whether it is reasonable to introduce such incentives before their likely effects on banking structure have been carefully investigated.

**3. Interest Rate Risk and Credit Risk.**    The effort to integrate interest rate risk and credit risk implies that these risks can be viewed as comparable. There are in reality, however, some important differences from both regulatory and banking points of view. The limits to which capital requirements can be effective in meeting regulatory objectives has already been discussed. No such limits exist, in concept, with respect to credit risk.

Beyond the regulatory limitations, capital requirements for interest rate risk also affect bank portfolio management in different ways than they do for credit risk. With respect to credit risk, once the agencies establish more or less stable risk weights, banks can decide how much capital is optimal through a selection of assets and their volume. If the risk weights are realistic—and given their own risk preferences—decisions should efficiently reflect profit opportunities.

Interest rate risk, on the other hand, depends on interest rate volatility, which in turn depends on exogenous market factors beyond the control and, in general, the predictive ability of banks and regulators. Risk weights, such as those established by the agencies, may be relatively stable, but to the extent that they are they will not be realistic. On a practical basis, as noted, capital levels cannot be established within a time frame appropriate for asset-liability decision making. As a result, they will not be selected by banks, in making their portfolio decisions, but will be imposed by outside factors—that is, exogenously. The exogenous determination of incremental capital requirements raises questions about unexpected costs that could confront banks, particularly in the emergence of high–interest rate volatility regimes. It also raises questions about whether bank asset and liability decisions will efficiently reflect profit opportunities.

**4. Limits on Bank Supervision.**   If actual interest rate risk exposure is traceable to interest rate volatility and shifts and twists in the yield curve, the cyclical state of the economy, *ceteris paribus*, is a principal determinant. While the timing and extent of volatility changes are not, in general, predictable, the data we have reviewed indicate that they tend to rise in business contractions.

To the extent this experience can be relied on, regulators would need to insist on capital additions in an expansion in anticipation of capital erosion in the following recession. A need for additional capital emanating from increased credit risk in expansion has long been understood.[16] It may now be embedded in risk-based requirements.

It appears that interest rate risk may function in much the same way as expansion gives way to contraction. In the past, without any mechanism to increase capital as additional credit risk was incurred, supervisors were generally not successful in doing so. In fact, their views of risk have seemed to be  influenced as much as bankers' by current successes. With only expectational considerations regarding interest rate and bank equity volatility, it may be too much to ask of supervisors to increase their estimates of expected volatility as an expansion ages. In the past, the Federal Reserve, in conducting monetary policy, has been a principal source of changes in interest rate volatility. It is reasonable to ask how non–Federal Reserve supervisors (or even Federal Reserve supervisors) without adequate information about changes in Federal Reserve aims and methods realistically estimate the expected volatility of bank equity.

A final point can be made with regard to monetary policy. Changes in a policy regime (for example, from one that aims at establishing interest rate levels to another that ignores them by setting money supply targets only) has, in the past, been an important determinant of interest rate volatility. Is it reasonable to make banks pay for the cost of such changes through additions to capital?

Effectiveness, incentive, and other policy questions are particularly significant in light of the fact that commercial banks have never experienced S&L-type interest-rate risk problems, even in the early 1980s, when interest rate volatility was enormous. Despite the concern about banks' substituting interest rate risk for credit risk, no urgent need for integrating interest rate risk into risk-based capital requirements has been established. The questions that arise can be obviated by arbitrary appraisals, but only at the cost of arbitrary results.

## ALTERNATIVES

The deficiencies of the current approach, both for the agencies and for banks, suggest consideration of alternatives for controlling interest rate risk. Implicit in the legislation and the agencies' several proposals is the view that additional capital is necessary for this purpose.

### Supervisory Intervention through Capital Assessments

The September 1993 proposal (Federal Reserve Board, September 1993) would have triggered supervisory intervention if the IRR index exceeded a threshold of 1.0 percent, that is, if there were an index level indicating a reduction in a bank's economic equity value–to–assets ratio of more than 1.0 percent as a result of a ±200 basis point change in interest rates.[17] The 1995 rule and Policy statement do not go so far, but still contemplate the use of a capital charge to offset excess exposure. Alternative methods for assessing a bank's capital adequacy for interest rate risk are proposed. However, all use bank capital as the principal instrument to achieve interest rate risk control.

### Alternative Modeling Approaches

**Office of Thrift Supervision (OTS) Approach.**    The Office of Thrift Supervision (OTS) has developed a methodology that it refers to as the "OTS Net Portfolio Value Model."[18] This approach attempts to estimate the effect of parallel shifts in the yield curve of interest rate changes of ±100 bp, ± 200 bp, ±300 bp, and ±400 bp on the value of individual assets, liabilities, and off–balance sheet contracts (Office of Thrift Supervision, 1994, pp. 1–1, 1–4). This form of "stress testing," as the OTS refers to its scenario analysis, forces thrift regulators and managers to evaluate the consequences of events that may be so extreme as to be ignored under normal conditions. Fundamentally, the approach attempts to measure the effects of interest rate changes, given the current portfolio of assets, liabilities, and off–balance sheet contracts, at the end of each quarter for each reporting thrift.[19] From a base case net asset value, calculated by the OTS from the reported portfolio positions, the OTS estimates the changes in the net asset value for each of the prescribed interest rate scenarios.

In effect, the OTS approach attempts to "mark-to-market" the balance sheet of each thrift for each interest rate scenario to determine the net portfolio value (NPV) for that scenario. This is defined, for scenario $j$, as:[20]

$$
NPV_j \equiv
\begin{array}{ll}
+ & \text{Present value of expected net cash flows} \\
  & \text{from each asset for scenario } j \\
- & \text{Present value of expected net cash flows} \\
  & \text{for each liability for scenario } j \\
+ & \text{Present value of net expected cash flows} \\
  & \text{from off–balance sheet contracts for scenario } j
\end{array}
\qquad (1)
$$

Greater risk exposure is implied by a larger change in the NPV for a given interest rate change scenario.

An important element for S&Ls in evaluating interest rate change effects is the embedded prepayment option of mortgages and mortgage backed securities (MBS).[21] The OTS modeling approach estimates the value of these instruments by employing the "option adjusted spread" (OAS) methodology, which measures the effective discount rate as the return on a nonoption instrument (usually a U.S. Treasury security) plus the value of the put option based on industry-produced information. This approach is practically the same as the one adopted by the bank regulators for the 1995 IRR implementation for banks (see Office of the Comptroller, 1995a).

Unlike the banking agencies' 1995 approach, the OTS imposes a capital assessment on those banks not meeting risk-based capital standards after adjusting for interest rate risk. The OTS incorporates an interest rate risk component (IRR component) into its risk-based capital standards for those institutions with greater than "normal" levels of interest rate risk. The "normal" level of interest rate risk for an institution is when its measured IRR is less than 2.0 percent. Measured IRR is defined as the change in NPV for a particular interest rate scenario as a percentage of the present value of assets (PVA) in the base case:

$$\text{Measured IRR}_j \equiv \frac{\text{NPV}_{\text{base}} - \text{NPV}_{\text{scenario } j}}{\text{PVA}_{\text{base}}} \tag{2}$$

The interest rate scenario generating the largest value of measured IRR is the case that is used for assessing the IRR component to capital.

If the measured IRR exceeds 2.0 percent, the interest rate risk capital component is calculated as one-half the excess of the measured IRR above 2.0 percent times the base case present value of assets. This computation is as follows:

$$\text{IRR capital component} \equiv \left[ \frac{\text{Max measured IRR} - 0.02}{2} \right] \tag{3}$$

The OTS risk-based capital rule allows S&Ls to use the lowest IRR capital component of those (based on reports of the three preceding quarters) to determine the capital required to cover interest rate risk. This amount would be deducted from an S&L's total capital in computing its risk-based capital ratio.

The OTS approach is fundamentally the same as the banking agencies' approach published in 1993 and revised by them as the "supervisory model" in August 1995. It relies heavily on the "duration" approach as discussed in Chapter 5 and is subject to the same criticisms. It has a further flaw that we have discussed, and that is the ad hoc nature of translating interest rate risk into a capital assessment consistent with a risk-based capital structure developed to assess default risk. It is with this criticism that the next section deals.

**Risk Capital Approach to Risk Management and Capital Assessments.**    Modern financial theory, as embodied in the Modigliani and Miller (1958 and 1963) (M&M) and the capital asset pricing model (CAPM) paradigms, provides a foundation to understand the role leverage can play in bank prudential supervision. From the CAPM, greater leverage raises the cost of equity capital. Controlling leverage increases the weighted average cost of capital beyond the firm's desired level—an imposed capital constraint is binding. Such leverage restrictions may increase the incentive for the bank to undertake more risky asset allocations to overcome the higher costs of capital. The result would be a bank *with a higher systematic risk component (beta) and a riskier portfolio.* Therefore, a binding capital constraint establishes an incentive for the firm to invest in riskier assets. Thus, if the intent of the supervisor is to control risk exposure, a risk-based capital standard and a risk-based deposit insurance premium structure need to be established coincident with binding capital constraints in the form of greater capital requirements imposed by bank supervisors.

Assumptions about the nature of information and about management-specialized knowledge and skill in the M&M and CAPM paradigms create different reasons to believe that internal risk management can influence the value of the firm. Bank managers have acquired skills and risk management systems that have become well developed and are far superior to those of the average investor. Just as important, however, is the nature of the business of banking. Principally, it is a risk management business with customers that rely on bankers' expertise to provide them with financial advice and support for their business, professional, and personal needs.

Bank customers purchase financial services and are the primary liability holders of the bank. They demand banking services (loans, lines of credit, payment services, financial planning, etc.) that are delivered risk-free. The business of banking is to provide customers with these services with little risk to the value of deposits or to meeting credit needs (e.g., loan commitments). Accordingly, banks have an incentive to maintain high credit and reputation. To do so requires the resources to meet commitments unwaveringly and to absorb losses on assets without disrupting their customers' financial condition.

The implication of these relationship characteristics is that banks require either an investment of equity capital to support customers against asset value volatility or must purchase asset or liability insurance from third parties. For many firms, one such third party consists of liability holders willing to accept higher returns for taking on the risks of default on the firms' debts. For banks this is largely not an acceptable source of insurance—namely, self-insurance by the liability holders. In banking, federal deposit insurance and the Federal Reserve's discount window provide significant depositor guarantees. An additional guarantee is the "too-big-to-fail" policy of bank regulators that provides direct support to the very largest banking companies and averts systemic declines in bank asset and liability values.[22] These factors lower the cost of capital for banks from what it otherwise would be to satisfy customers' demands for a stable source of funds.

An additional factor contributing to the need for bank capital and the high cost of capital is the degree of "opaqueness" of bank operations to outside investors and customers (see Merton and Perold, 1993, and Ross, 1989). Opaqueness arises especially with lending activities and bilateral agreements such as swaps. High degrees of opaqueness give rise to high monitoring and information costs to customers and investors (adverse selection and moral hazard), which, in turn, are responsible for high agency costs. Banks, and other financial firms, are able to quickly and almost undetectably change their asset structures to take more risky and event-susceptible portfolios than other firms. The implication of these factors is that capital must be available to cover these risks and risk management is integral to the strategic and operations management of banks.

The credit-quality sensitivity of bank customers and the high information and agency costs arising from opaqueness are one cause of banks' having higher capital costs than other financial firms such as mutual funds. Additionally, banks are largely multiproduct/multimarket firms offering services that are increasingly more competitive. The increasing competition is reflected in narrowing margins on all banking services. These competitive pressures make banks' profitability ever more sensitive to capital costs, particularly the costs of providing capital to absorb risks of asset and liability volatility (see Merton and Perold, 1993, p. 17). To some extent, these costs are reduced by the presence of federal government guarantees, such as federal deposit insurance and Federal Reserve discount and stabilization policies, including too-big-to-fail. However, competition and pressures on profitability make effective risk management an important method of controlling the high capital costs faced by banks.

Risk Capital: A Methodology for Measuring and Monitoring Bank Capital Needs. So far, a case has been made that the imposition of capital standards by bank supervisors requires that these be risk-based in order to avoid allowing banks to simply change their asset mix toward riskier assets in response to more stringent capital requirements. These problems of moral hazard are endemic to imposing essentially higher capital costs on banks. Second, it has been argued that banks, like many other financial intermediaries that act as principals to financial transactions (e.g., direct lenders, counterparties), need to promote themselves as low-risk enterprises to their customers and investors. This implies that to be competitive, they must be able to provide insurance on their assets such that their liabilities and other commitments are comparatively default-free—their customers do not bear a substantial portion of the risk of a bank's asset default. If banks did not follow such a course, the opaqueness of their operations and investments would mean high costs to their customers—largely liability holders or counterparties—and make them no more competitive for capital than any other firm.

With this as background, the question becomes, What is the required amount of equity capital necessary in order for banks to be competitive and profitable? Equivalently, what is the cost that bank owners will have to bear in order to provide the insurance on bank assets—risk management methods—necessary to permit them to be profitable and competitive? Merton and Perold (1993, p. 17) have provided an answer that develops the notion of "risk capital" as the "smallest amount that can be invested to insure the value of the firm's net assets against a loss in value relative to the risk-free investment of those assets."[23] The term risk-free means default risk–free in this context. "Net assets" are the market value of assets less the default-free equivalent value of liabilities and other commitments.

In a risk-capital balance sheet structure, the amount of risk capital for a given amount of risky assets, $A$, is:

$$\text{Risk capital} = \begin{matrix}\text{Market}\\\text{value of}\\\text{risky}\\\text{assets}\end{matrix} + \begin{matrix}\text{Asset}\\\text{insurance}\end{matrix} - \begin{matrix}\text{Default-}\\\text{free}\\\text{liability}\\\text{value}\end{matrix} - \begin{matrix}\text{Equity}\\\text{cash}\\\text{capital}\end{matrix} \qquad (4)$$

Asset insurance is composed of three sources:

1. The discounts from default-free values of liabilities
2. Third-party asset insurance premium values
3. Residual premiums supplied by shareholders, or the sale of asset insurance to the firm

"Default-free liability value" is the value of liabilities discounted at the default-free rate of interest. If liabilities are default risk–free, as would be federally insured deposits at banks, their value would be the same as book value. "Equity cash capital" is the contribution by equityholders such that the sum of this and default-free liabilities is equal to the market value of assets.

Risk capital is, by this definition, the residual amount determined by the riskiness of the net asset value of the firm. In contrast, cash capital is determined by the value of assets of the firm and is simply the sum of default-free liability value plus an equity value to equal asset value (Merton and Perold, 1993, p. 23). Essentially, then, risk capital is the amount necessary to provide asset insurance so as to make liabilities default risk–free. By the condition that liabilities are valued at their default-free value, the amount of risk capital required is independent of the form of financing of net assets (Merton and Perold, 1993, p. 30).

Risk capital according to Merton and Perold is the value of a European put option on the net asset value of the firm with a strike price equal to the future value of the initial net assets paying the default-free rate of return. This conception yields the same amount as the cost of asset insurance sufficient to repay liabilities at contractual values (including interest and other commitments) rather than default-free amounts. Thus, the risk capital value is related to the investment of initial net asset values at the default-free returns. Algebraically, the value of the payoff of this insurance is:[24]

$$\text{Insurance payoff} = \max[(A_0 - L_0) \exp(r_f T) - (A_T - L_T), 0] \qquad (5)$$

where:

| | | |
|---|---|---|
| $T$ | = | Terminal or maturity date of the liabilities |
| $A_t$ | = | Gross market value of assets at $t$ |
| $L_t$ | = | Default-free liability value at $t$ |

$L_T$ = Contractual value or par value of liabilities at $T$

$r_f$ = Default-free rate of return

Assuming geometric Brownian motion for gross assets and liability values, the put option can be valued using the Black-Scholes (1973) option pricing model. The value of the put option is the insurance premium and is the same as risk capital. Merton and Perold present an approximation for this value as:

$$\text{Risk capital} = (0.4)A_0 \, \sigma \sqrt{T} \tag{6}$$

where $\sigma$ is the volatility of profits on assets.[25]

The implication of this measure of risk capital is that it represents the minimum premium on asset insurance to guarantee the payoff of liabilities at their par value at maturity.[26] Risk management is the method by which such insurance is provided in banking, and the concept of risk capital is an attempt to measure the minimum cost of risk management.

For the purposes of evaluating interest rate risk in this risk-capital framework, it is important to identify three separate risks: default or credit risk, interest rate risk, and market risk (e.g., fluctuations in foreign exchange). Interest rate volatility as a source of risk to a bank is directly translatable into the valuation of risk capital in this model. For example, if credit and market risks for investments such as foreign exchange are ignored or held constant, the source of volatility, $\sigma$, is strictly due to volatility in interest rate changes. Consequently, the risk-capital approach is consistent with the stochastic modeling methodology presented in Chapter 5 and provides a systematic way of translating interest rate volatility into minimum capital requirements.

**Alternative Approaches to Measurement of Capital Adequacy for Risk Management Purposes.** As discussed above, bank supervisors have chosen bank capital, defined in various ways for reasons that are poorly specified in the regulations promulgated by the regulatory agencies, as the main instrument for supervising bank risk taking. Employing the concept of risk capital as the measure of the minimum cost necessary to manage risk, bank management can establish the required costs to meet the risk needs of their customers profitably. As a measure of the costs of providing asset insurance, it provides regulators with the information that is necessary to establish a capital requirement to meet their risk-taking standards for the bank—namely, the cost of the insurance or hedge to meet liability and other commitments at par.

In contrast to risk capital, a number of measures of capital requirements have been recently recommended for purposes of public and supervisory reporting and applying regulatory capital charges. One such method discussed above is value at risk, or VaR, as proposed by the Basle Committee on Banking Supervision (April 15, 1995). As defined for the purposes of this proposal, value at risk is a measure of market risk exposure and is an estimate of the likely maximum amount that could be lost on a bank's portfolio with a certain degree of statistical confidence (99 percent for this proposal) over a specified time horizon (two weeks for this proposal). The portfolio that this proposal is applied to is the trading portfolio of securities and derivative products (swaps, forward rate agreements, futures, etc.) on financial contracts and commodities. The capital charge for losses, after netting, will be to multiply the bank's VaR estimate by 3 and add on an amount for credit risk. This final result is some estimate of the amount required to "neutralize" or hedge the position giving rise to the estimate of VaR and to recognize this in supervisory capital.

Unlike risk capital, VaR is not a measure of the cost of providing insurance to liability holders. It only measures the extent of the loss up to some probability limit and over a short time horizon. The ad hoc choice of the factor of 3 multiple is an attempt to estimate the cost of the guarantee for the VaR estimated level of risk.

It should also be recognized that this capital charge is in addition to the risk-based capital charges as presented in Table 6–1. Consequently, a bank will be required to estimate numerous capital charges, each related in some way to its asset and liability structure (whether on or off balance sheet). As presented in Table 6–1 and as evidenced in the "3 times the estimated VaR value plus an add-on for default risk" rule as proposed by the Basle Committee on Banking Supervision, these capital rules are ad hoc and have little analytic or empirical foundation.

## TABLE 6–1
*Risk-Based Capital: Summary of Risk Weights and Major Assets in Each Risk Category*

*Category 1: 0% weight*

Cash

Balances due from Federal Reserve Banks and claims on central banks in other OECD coutries*

U.S. Treasury and government agency securities and claims on or unconditionally guaranteed by OECD central governments

Federal Reserve stock

Claims collateralized by cash on deposit or by securities issued or guaranteed by OECD central governments or U.S. government agencies

*Category 2: 20% weight*

Cash items in the process of collection

All claims on or guaranteed by U.S. depository institutions and banks in OECD countries

General obligation bonds of state and local governments

Portions of claims secured by U.S. government agency securities or OECD central government obligations that do not qualify for a 0% weight

Loans or other claims conditionally guaranteed by the U.S. government

Securities and other claims on U.S. government–sponsored agencies

*Category 3: 50% weight*

Loans secured by first liens on 1- to 4-family residential property and certain multifamily residential properties

Certain privately issued mortgage-backed securities

Revenue bonds of state and local governments

*Category 4: 100% weight*

All loans and other claims on private obligors not placed in a lower risk category

Bank premises, fixed assets, and other real estate owned

Industrial development revenue bonds

Intangible assets and investment in unconsolidated subsidiaries, provided they are not deducted from capital

---

*The group of countries associated with the Organization for Economic Cooperation and Development (OECD) includes the United States and 24 other major industrial countries.

The risk-based capital requirements are a "one-size-fits-all" approach without any recognition of the fact that banks are multi-product/multimarket firms with complex interactions of payoffs on their assets and other business commitments. In comparison to the risk capital approach presented in this paper, the risk-based capital standards are imperfect and imprecise and may be misstating the amount of capital required by some banks. Little recognition is given, in a quantitative way, to risk management by banks and the methods that they can take to best control the costs of risk to the bank's liability holders and the FDIC. An example may best explain the inadequacies of the risk-based capital system.

Consider two banks with the same market value of risky assets, but with different mixes. Bank A has $1 billion in assets with 30 percent invested in business loans, and bank B has the same amount of assets but with 30 percent in real estate development loans on commercial properties. Each of these loans is 100 percent risk-weighted, and the banks have all other asset categories and liabilities the same. The volatility of business loan value is expected to be about 30 percent per year, that of loans on commercial properties is 60 percent per year, and volatility on all other assets is 20 percent per year. There is a correlation among the changes in market value of these and other assets in the portfolio, but they are assumed to be positive and small enough to ignore. The volatility for bank A, $\sigma_A$, is 16.6 percent:

$$\sigma_A = \sqrt{(0.7^2)\sigma_o^2 + (0.3^2)\,\sigma_b^2} = 0.166$$

where $\sigma_b$ is the volatility for business loans and $\sigma_o$ is the volatility for other banking assets. Similarly, the volatility for bank B is 22.8 percent per year. Employing the approximation to the Black-Scholes model, the value of risk capital to assets for bank A is 6.64 percent, and for bank B it is 9.12 percent. Using the risk-based system, each bank would have the same capital requirements to be well capitalized, while the two banks' risk capital differs considerably, with bank B needing 37 percent more capital. Assuming both banks have the same ratio of Tier-1 capital to risk-based assets of 6 percent, bank B may be severely undercapitalized from a risk management perspective compared with bank A. Since the risk-based capital standards make no distinction between these two banks, it is left to the examiners to criticize bank B's lending policies, a clear failure of the risk-based capital system to automatically constrain bank risk taking.

**A Comparison of Effects on Bank Management Incentives to Manage Risk.** The incentive structure of risk-based capital supervisory standards has not been well explored. Although, as discussed above, the standards have a general foundation in financial economic theory, there has been little research on the effects on bank behavior and performance resulting from the adoption of these standards. Research that has reviewed the credit crunch that occurred at about the same time, FDICIA imposed "prompt corrective action" seems to reveal banks' willingness to adopt more restrictive lending policies in order to reduce capital requirements. Alternatively, the recession and collapse of the commercial real estate markets in the Northeast and Mid-Atlantic regions of the United States and in some foreign markets may have been a greater incentive to restrict lending. Kupiec and O'Brien (1995b) consider an alternative to a rigid risk-based capital approach to establishing supervisory capital standards. Their approach, although developed to apply to capital standards for banks that use their internal models as proposed by the Basle Committee on Banking Supervision (1995) for market risks, has applicability for any system of capital charges that allows banks to use internal models for risk assessment. As recognized by the Basle Committee, the supervisors' choice of an internal approach to risk assessment should be better aligned with the banks' own systems for risk analysis and control and reduce the potential costs from the distortion in banks' portfolio choices due to rigidity in the ad hoc risk-based weighting of banking activities.

Since there are serious problems of measurement and verification of the internal models approach for market risk exposures (see Kupiec and O'Brien, 1995a), and considerable questions of the current risk-based capital standards approach, Kupiec and O'Brien propose the following pre-commitment approach:

. . . banks would pre-commit to a maximum potential loss exposure on their trading portfolio over the regulatory holding period and would then be requested to set aside enough capital to cover their maximum loss pre-commitment. Penalties would be assessed for a violation of the maximum loss pre-commitment *sic, (cumulatively over the regulatory holding period).* The penalties might take the form of additional capital charges or pecuniary fines but could also include other supervisory actions. If designed properly, such penalties would create strong incentives for a going-concern bank to adhere to its maximum loss commitment. . . . While the bank itself would choose its capital commitment, both the commitment and the bank's risk management systems would be subject to review by supervisory authorities who would have to be satisfied that the pre-commitment was consistent with the trading policy and risk management controls of the bank (Kupiec and O'Brien, 1995b, pp. 2–3).

The benefits of this approach are threefold. First, it explicitly places the risk management system of the bank as the assessor of maximum potential loss. Second, it proposes that penalties, if properly designed, serve to correct tendencies for risky trading practices to be perpetuated. And third, this same incentive structure provides for capitalization consistent with trading practices adopted to attain the risk management goals.

These benefits indicate the fundamental differences in this approach from the risk-based capital approach presently used by the banking regulators. However, it retains the bank supervisor as a risk manager by specifying a supervisory determined penalty function. This function is conditional on a supervisory stipulated likelihood that the capital commitment will be violated—namely, a realized loss that is greater than the pre-commitment value (Kupiec and O'Brien, 1995b, pp. 6–7). Thus, finding a penalty function and method of charging (e.g., increased capital, monetary fine, or stricter supervisory oversight) that is incentive-compatible, such that the bank would choose the same or greater capital backing for a given exposure, is the element of this plan that produces the benefits. For example, if the penalty charge is too high, the bank will set risk exposure levels high enough that it will never experience a penalty, knowing full well that the risk exposure will never be violated. In contrast, if the penalties are set too low, the bank will set low risk exposure levels and violate them continually. In the first example, the bank will have to keep a greater capital position that will tend to raise its capital costs if it does not have excess capital. In the second case of too low penalties, the bank will face the possibility of being insufficiently capitalized at just the time when it may need more capital.

The risk-capital methodology in measuring the cost of providing asset insurance presented above may help to contribute to the establishment of the penalty prescription in the pre-commitment approach. In the risk-capital method, the penalty rate would be the cost of providing the hedge or buying asset insurance against the exposure of a particular trading position taken by the bank. This is the risk capital calculation presented above (equation 4). It depends on the characteristics of the position or on the bank's risk asset composition, if the position is the bank's total assets. The cost of the hedge or insurance depends on the composition of the loss being generated—some types of losses can be more efficiently hedged than others. Consequently, under the risk capital method of setting the amount of capital necessary to insure a particular position, positions with the same value of loss need not have the same cost of insurance. Therefore, banks could use their risk management expertise to achieve an optimal insurance strategy without the regulator specifying the same penalty rate for every type of position.

**Stochastic Modeling Approach.** The stochastic modeling approach presented in Chapter 5 is an attempt to place dynamic interest rate changes into the determination of interest rate risk on bank market values. This approach focuses attention on the change in the volatility of interest rates and the impact of that volatility on bank equity. As was shown, interest rates behave differently in high- versus low-volatility regimes, and each type of behavior poses different risks for banks. The inability to accurately predict periods of low versus high interest rate volatility creates its own set of risks that are not considered in any of the approaches presented by the bank regulators to date.

Employing a stochastic approach to the problem of interest rate risk would be more reasonable for banks and also provide better protection for the deposit insurance fund. It would be consistent with FDICIA to require an addition to total capital when the likelihood of capital erosion exceeds some threshold value. The amount of capital erosion that seems relevant, under FDICIA's "prompt corrective action" rule, is the amount that would reduce capital so as to move a bank from one category to a lower one (e.g., from well capitalized to adequately capitalized; see Table 1–3 in Chapter 1) and, in particular, to levels that would place a bank in one of the three "undercapitalized" categories. Of course, the difficult problem that remains is to accurately determine which interest rate volatility regime will prevail until the next examination in order to measure the bank's interest rate risk exposure for the current period. If the regulator picks the wrong regime, the bank may suffer a capital deficiency and incur excessive interest rate risk exposure or, alternatively, be forced to incur unnecessary capital costs.

The use of the stochastic measures of interest rate risk exposure suggests the greater use of detailed, bank-specific information in a stochastic scenario analysis and less reliance on gross approximations; the analysis might best be undertaken by individual banks for their own benefit. Furthermore, the analysis needs to be done daily, and intraday for volatile portfolios, in order to confidently monitor whether interest rate risk exposure has increased. It also encourages on-site supervisory evaluations of the analytical methods and scenarios of interest rate volatility used by banks to assess interest rate risk and, where detailed data can be utilized, without imposing excessive reporting burdens on banks. Most importantly, it provides an incentive structure for banks to better monitor and control interest rate risk. From the regulators' perspective, the capital adequacy standards for interest rate risk would then directly focus on the likelihood of bank capital impairment and on the bank's management of its interest rate risk exposure rather than on an arbitrary level of an index established by agency rule making.

## CONCLUSIONS: UNFINISHED BUSINESS

FDICIA was passed, as FIRREA before it, in large part because of the impact bank failure and potential failure had on the federal deposit insurance funds. Reliance on risk-based capital requirements and prompt corrective action (PCA) has been an exercise in protecting the deposit insurance funds and, beyond the funds, the taxpayer. Integrating interest rate risk into risk-based capital requirements is meant to serve this end.

Why, then, have the agencies been so sluggish in imposing requirements on a systematic basis? The long delay in establishing a "rule," and the partial nature of the rule, indicate the difficulties involved in incorporating interest rate risk into risk-based capital requirements. The difficulties further suggest important implications for public policy.

The proposal of the federal banking agencies to revise risk-based capital standards to incorporate interest rate risk reflects continuing efforts under FDICIA to protect the deposit insurance fund from a repeat of recent experience. It also reflects a move toward market-based capital requirements by attempting to account for changes in the economic value of bank equity resulting from changes in market interest rates.

The effort to develop a more realistic approach to measuring interest rate risk for purposes of risk-based capital requirements (in a stochastic framework) opened a Pandora's box of technical and policy issues. The agencies' abandonment, for the time being, of the minimum capital standards approach has left them with a measuring scheme that, per se, has no implications for what is too much or too little interest rate risk, and for what is too little or too much capital to meet this risk. They have been extraordinarily, but properly, cautious in establishing a formal set of "rules" for requiring more capital. An opportunity now exists to consider alternatives for safeguarding banks, such as those discussed above.

## Appendix
### Why Did It Take So Long to Do So Little?

The problem of interest rate risk, as noted in earlier chapters, was apparent by the mid-1960s. The effort to incorporate interest rate risk exposure into risk-based capital requirements began in the mid to late 1980s at the federal banking agencies, and earlier among thrift supervisors. The devastating impact of interest rate volatility on thrifts in the early 1980s was no doubt influential. The establishment of new capital standards in the mid-1980s by the federal agencies, the recognition that banks could subvert them by taking greater risks, and the Basle agreement to establish risk-based capital requirements in the late 1980s established a foundation for incorporating interest rate risk. It was apparent to those working on risk-based requirements that if interest rate risk was not incorporated, it could be substituted for credit risk.

The federal banking agencies, then, have had the problem on their agenda for roughly 30 years. They have worked seriously on the problem for about 10 years, and for the last 4 or 5 years under the pressure of a statutory deadline. One might have expected a complete and thorough system as a result. The "Final Rule" and "policy statement" of August 1995, as noted, do little more than formalize what has been long understood—that is, that the federal banking agencies have the authority to require that banks add capital for interest rate risk and that they will use various types of relevant information in reaching decisions as to how much is needed. These results, after about a decade in which the problem has been understood and five or so years of serious effort, raise the question of why so little has been accomplished.

## The Agencies' Explanation

The agencies have provided a partial explanation for their sluggishness. In issuing their Joint Agency Policy Statement in August 1995, they explained that "the delay reflects the difficult tradeoffs the banking agencies have faced in developing and implementing a rule that provides a sufficiently accurate basis for estimating banks' interest rate risk exposure and their need for capital, yet maintains enough transparency and simplicity to allow bank management to readily determine their regulatory capital requirements" (Summary, Joint Agency Policy Statement, August 1995, p. 4). In other words, they struggled with developing rules that were practical. In the end, they concluded that they did not have any.

The agencies also indicate that "the difficulties have been magnified by the rapid pace of change in financial markets and instruments themselves" (Introduction, Joint Agency Policy Statement, August 1995, p. 6). In other words, it is difficult to know how to evaluate some of the new instruments with respect to their interest rate risk and determine how much capital is needed in support of them. The bank regulators conceded that "Because of different measurement systems and management philosophies, the measured exposure of banks may not be directly comparable." (Joint Agency Policy Statement, August 1995, p. 6.)

The agencies concluded that "it is appropriate to first collect industry data and evaluate the performance of the measurement framework before explicitly incorporating the results of that framework into their risk-based capital standards" (Introduction, Joint Agency Policy Statement, p. 9). Reading between the lines suggests that the federal banking agencies found the task of designing a systematic approach to incorporating interest rate risk a difficult problem. As noted, the agencies may have the wrong paradigm in attempting to do so through risk-based capital requirements. Further, it appears that the several agencies could not agree on a variety of issues that arose. In this circumstance, it is not difficult to understand why.

## Is Interest Rate Risk a Problem for Commercial Banks?

There is nothing wrong with proceeding cautiously when problems are not imminent. The slowness in implementing systemic interest rate risk requirements (the minimum capital standards approach) might imply that the agencies do not perceive an immediate problem that needs to be solved. As noted, interest rate risk has not appeared in the past as a critical problem for commercial banks. Moreover, large banks seem to be dealing with it effectively, even though taking losses, from time to time, on securities. Finally, with monetary policy now aimed at low or zero inflation, the level and volatility of interest rates, at least for the near future, seems to be moderate.

This last point suggests the possible existence of an interest rate risk illusion, that is, that exposure to this kind of risk is not an imminent problem for banks. There is some danger, however, in projecting current conditions into the future. As noted in this chapter, changes in "volatility" and monetary policy "regimes" are unpredictable. But like the systemic events to which they are related, we can be reasonably certain that change will occur.

## NOTES

1. The agencies have contrasted the "minimum capital standard" with a "risk assessment" approach. In the latter approach, examiners are given discretion to consider a variety of factors, including the results of the supervisory and other models, in determining excess interest rate risk exposure and the resulting capital charge.
2. It also required that risk-based capital standards take into account concentration of credit risk, the risks of nontraditional activities, and also reflect the actual performance and expected risk of loss of multifamily mortgages.
3. A "Joint Advance Notice of Proposed Rulemaking" (ANPR) to take account of interest rate risk was published, for comment, on July 30,

1992 (Federal Reserve Board, 1992). The ANPR developed the measurement methodology, supervisory model, and minimum capital standards approach that subsequently was proposed in September 1993 (Federal Reserve Board, 1993).

4. Office of the Comptroller (1995a), p. 39490.

5. Ibid., p. 39491.

6. Ibid.

7. Office of the Comptroller (1995b), pp. 39495–571.

8. Office of the Comptroller (1995a), pp. 39491–492.

9. The 1993 NPR proposed to exempt from reporting requirements banks who, on the basis of their operations, did not seem seriously threatened by interest rate risk. These included those whose long-term loans and securities (maturing or repricing in 5 years or more) were such that 15 percent amounted to less than 30 percent of total capital; *and* also with off–balance sheet interest rate contracts (notional value) that did not exceed 10 percent of total assets. It was estimated on the basis of 1992 call report data that about 8,400 banks would meet these exemption standards (Federal Reserve Board, 1993, p. 20).

10. A parallel shift in the yield curve of 100 basis points for a quarterly time horizon and 200 basis points for a year would constitute a hypothetical shock to determine exposure. An instantaneous 200 basis point shift was used to illustrate the proposed rule.

11. It was proposed that a bank's exposure would be computed on each quarterly call date. The proposal called for banks to sustain their capital in accordance with their exposure continuously.

12. More precisely, the excess exposure of $1 million is multiplied by 12.5 (the reciprocal of the 8 percent ratio), and the resulting $12.5 million is added to the bank's risk-weighted assets. This addition would raise the bank's risk-weighted assets to $112.5 million and reduce its total risk-based capital ratio from 10 percent to 8.89 percent. Without additions to capital, the bank would fall from a well-capitalized status under the capital levels established by the agencies for prompt corrective action to adequately capitalized. If the bank's total capital had been only $8 million instead of $10 million, its risk-based capital ratio would have declined from 8 percent to 7.11 percent. As a result of its excess interest rate risk exposure, the bank would fall from an adequately capitalized status to undercapitalized. Without an addition to capital to restore the 8 percent ratio, it would be subject to serious regulatory intervention, including the need to file a capital restoration plan.

13. There are numerous issues discussed throughout the 1993 NPR that are generally applicable to any regulatory measurement, appraisal, and capital assessment system. Some of the more important are: (1) how to slot so-called nonmaturity deposits, i.e., transactions deposits and savings accounts, among the time bands available; (2) the appropriate interest rate change scenario, and its related time horizon, with which the interest rate risk exposure is determined; and (3) the acceptability, for supervisory purposes, of internal bank models as opposed to, or in conjunction with, the supervisory model. The proposal recognized that the response of nonmaturity deposits to interest rate changes can differ significantly from bank to bank, and that any specified slotting may have important effects on measured interest rate risk. It also recognized the arbitrary nature of the +200 bp parallel shift in the yield curve and some of its deficiencies. It was acknowledged that "scenario" revisions might have to be made periodically. Finally, the NPR acknowledged that some banks, particularly larger ones, might better evaluate their interest rate risk through their own internal models. It not only expressed a willingness to accept the results of internal bank models if they met supervisory standards, but indicated that they might be used by the agencies if they indicated a need for more capital than the results of the supervisory model.

14. A naive view would be that if +200 bp is insufficient, then +300 bp might be: Clearly, there is some hypothesized increase that would conceivably cover the worst-case possibility. This approach, of course, ignores the cost to banks of meeting capital requirements or other penalties to cover the worst-case scenario.

15. This comment was made by Walter B. Wriston in a 1992 op-ed piece in *The Wall Street Journal*, p. A-14.

16. This need emerges from the increasing fragility of banks during periods of expansion, and the tendency of bankers to ignore hazards of seemingly low probability. There have been a substantial number of papers and books on the subject in recent years. A paper by Hyman Minsky at the Federal Reserve Bank of Chicago in 1975 (pp. 150–84) was an early recognition of the problem. More recently, Jack Guttentag and Richard Herring provided a careful examination of the issues in "Disaster Myopia in International Banking" (September 1986).

17. The agency proposal permits a bank to use its internal risk measure" . . . for evaluating IRR when the methodology and key assumptions to that measure are deemed adequate by the appropriate

Banking Agency. . . . Banks would be expected to maintain appropriate internal risk measurement systems consistent with their risk profiles" (Federal Reserve Board, September 1993, p. 11).

18. See Office of Thrift Supervision (1994).

19. Participating thrifts report Schedule CMR of the Thrift Financial Report quarterly, and estimates of the effects of interest rate changes are based on the term structure at the end of the quarter (Office of Thrift Supervision, 1994, p. 1–2). Certain institutions are not required to file the Schedule CMR. These institutions are exempt from the IRR capital component of the risk-based capital requirements. Institutions with less than $300 million in assets and risk-based capital ratios above 12 percent are also exempt unless other conditions apply. Some institutions voluntarily file the Schedule CMR, but are not subject to interest rate risk capital assessments (Office of Thrift Supervision, 1994, p. 2A–3, footnote 6).

20. This approach assumes that certain expenses and revenues not related to interest rates, such as wages and deposit account fees, are constant and are treated as such in the NPV analysis.

21. Conceptually, S&L and bank deposits face a similar optionality component, since depositors can opt to withdraw their deposits if offered interest rates are below market-available returns (some index of deposit returns). For an individual depository, these deposits would flow out and the funds not return until they were attracted back by higher interest rates being offered.

22. With FDICIA (1991), the FDIC, the Federal Reserve, the Treasury Department, and the President must make a systemic finding for a bank about to fail to bypass the least-cost rule of bank disposition by the FDIC.

23. Merton and Perold (1993), p. 17.

24. Merton and Perold (1993), p. 31.

25. The volatility used by Merton and Perold in this approximation to the Black-Scholes model is the volatility of the percentage change in the ratio of gross assets to default-free liabilities, $A_t/L_t$, or the volatility of the percentage change in assets less the percentage change in liability values.

26. This notion is not much different than valuing a premium for federal deposit insurance as presented in Merton (1977). However, the put option is better related to the reasons for bankers to conduct active risk management.

# REFERENCES

Black, Fisher, and Myron Scholes. "The Pricing of Options and Corporate Liabilities," *Journal of Political Economy* 81, (May–June 1973), pp. 637–54.

Federal Reserve Board, Press Release, *Interagency Advance Notice of Proposed Rulemaking to Revise Risk-Based Capital Standards*, July 30, 1992.

Federal Reserve Board, Press Release, *Interagency Notice of Proposed Rulemaking to Revise Risk-Based Capital Standards*, September 14, 1993.

Guttentag, Jack, and Richard Herring. "Disaster Myopia in International Banking," *Essays in International Finance*, No. 164, International Finance Section, Princeton University, September 1986, p. 33.

Kupiec, Paul H., and James M. O'Brien (1995a). "Internal Affairs," *Risk* 8, no. 5 (May 1995), pp. 18–20.

Kupiec, Paul H., and James M. O'Brien (1995b). "A Pre-Commitment Approach to Capital Requirements for Market Risk," draft, Board of Governors of the Federal Reserve System, April 1995.

Merton, Robert C. "An Analytical Derivation of the Cost of Deposit Insurance and Loan Guarantees: An Application of Modern Option Pricing Theory," *Journal of Banking and Finance* 1 (June 1977), pp. 3–11.

Merton, Robert C., and André F. Perold. "Theory of Risk Capital in Financial Firms," Continental Bank *Journal of Applied Corporate Finance* 6 (Fall 1993), pp. 16–32.

Minsky, Hyman P. "Suggestions for a Cash-Flow Oriented Bank Examinations," *Proceedings of a Conference on Bank Structure and Competition*, Federal Reserve Bank of Chicago, 1975, pp. 150–84.

Modigliani, Franco, and Merton Miller. "The Cost of Capital, Corporation Finance, and the Theory of Investment," *American Economic Review* (June 1958), pp. 261–97.

Modigliani, Franco, and Merton Miller. "Taxes and the Cost of Capital: A Correction," *American Economic Review* (June 1963), pp. 433–43.

Office of the Comptroller of the Currency, Federal Reserve System, and FDIC (1995a). "Risk Based Capital Standards: Interest Rate Risk: Final Rule" *"Federal Register*, (Rules and Regulations) 60, no. 148 (August 2, 1995), pp. 39490–39494.

Office of the Comptroller of the Currency, Federal Reserve System, and FDIC (1995b). "Joint Agency Policy Statement: Supervisory Policy

Statement Concerning a Supervisory Framework for Measuring and Assessing Banks' Interest Rate Risk Exposure," *Federal Register* (Proposed Rules) 60, no. 148 (August 2, 1995), pp. 39495–39571.

Office of Thrift Supervision, *The OTS Net Portfolio Value Model,* Risk Management Division, Office of Thrift Supervision, Washington, D.C., November 1994.

Ross, Stephen. "Institutional Markets, Financial Marketing, and Financial Innovation," *Journal of Finance* 44 (July 1989), pp. 541–56.

Spong, Kenneth. *Banking Regulation: Its Purposes, Implementations, and Effects.* 4th ed. Federal Reserve Bank of Kansas City, 1994.

Wriston, Walter B. "Bank Weaknesses Are a Regulatory Illusion," *The Wall Street Journal,* February 7, 1992, p. A–14.

# Chapter Seven

# The Future of Interest Rate Risk: Findings and Prospects

Interest rate changes threaten bank earnings and their market value. The principal examples in recent memory were the interest rate increases of the late 1970s and early 1980s, which were the proximate cause of the subsequent S&L disaster. More recently, interest rate risk has threatened individual banks with susceptible off–balance sheet activities and investment portfolios skewed toward long-term instruments.

FDICIA requires the federal banking agencies to incorporate interest rate risk into existing risk-based capital requirements. Congress and the federal banking agencies currently see interest rate risk as a threat to the federal deposit insurance funds. Of course, banks, themselves, need to manage their interest rate risk exposure independently of regulatory requirements.

The effectiveness of recently established, and still evolving, interest rate risk regulations will depend on whether analysis of the problem is valid and the proposed solution can be established without excessive costs of one kind or another. The approach now taken by the agencies (and the Basle Committee) is that interest rate risk can be translated into a credit risk equivalent, and subjected to an appropriate capital charge. This capital charge must be large enough to provide bank supervisors with "sufficient comfort" that interest rate risk exposure does not pose a risk to individual banks beyond their capacity to manage it and pose a meaningful level of systemic risk. The methodology for the translation has, however, been difficult to establish. There are reasons to believe that the basic approach overextends the capability of capital requirements as an instrument in supervising risk taking.

In the preceding chapters, we have examined the emergence of interest rate risk as both a bank problem and a regulatory problem, and the development of capital requirements as the principal tool of bank regulation. We have reviewed the techniques for measuring and modeling interest rate risk, in particular, the techniques proposed by the federal banking agencies. We have examined key issues related to the still incomplete efforts of the agencies to integrate interest rate risk into risk-based capital requirements. It is helpful, at this point, to briefly review our principal findings, to project what the future may be for interest rate risk and its regulation, and to propose how banks and the banking agencies should deal with the problems that will continue to exist.

## REVIEW OF FINDINGS

Over the past century, interest rates have raised various kinds of economic and financial issues. Rising interest rates, falling interest rates, and fluctuating and even stable interest rates have been viewed, at different times, as serious problems. Until the last 30 years or so, however, interest rate risk, as currently understood, was not considered a serious practical problem for commercial banks.

It became such a problem, particularly for savings institutions, as a result of changes in economic and institutional conditions, in particular, rising interest rates, increasing competition for deposit funds, and weakening regulatory constraints on deposit rates of interest. By the mid-1960s, the impact of sharp increases in interest rates on S&Ls and savings banks was reasonably clear. At that time, Regulation Q interest rate ceilings on deposits were usually modified by the bank regulatory agencies to accommodate market interest rate changes. By the early 1980s, the persistence of the problem and the potential effect on all depository institutions was undeniably apparent. The rising interest rates of the 1970s, triggered by the oil embargoes' effects on inflation, and the high interest rates of the early 1980s left many S&Ls with negative net worth on a present value basis. The result was a serious moral hazard problem facing the deposit insurers.

The growing awareness among bank regulators of interest rate risk was paralleled by a movement to constrain what regulators believed to be excessive risk taking through more exacting capital requirements. Financial markets alone, this belief implied, could not be relied on to require capital in an amount appropriate to the risks undertaken. This result could be traced to the absence of publicly available and timely information on the condition of banks, and also to support provided banks by the federal "safety net" that included deposit insurance and the Federal Reserve's discount window.

Capital requirements were redesigned as a regulatory tool, with first "minimum" and then risk-based standards established. New requirements for savings institutions were established by the Financial Institutions Reform, Recovery, and Enforcement Act of 1989 (FIRREA), and graduated intervention and restrictions for failure to meet them ("prompt corrective action") were established by the FDIC Improvement Act of 1991 (FDICIA).

The resurrection of capital requirements has not been simply domestic, but has been international in scope, a necessary condition for a "level playing field" for large, international banking organizations. From the regulatory perspective in a risk-based capital environment, interest rate risk *must* be incorporated, because otherwise banks could trade off credit risk, for which capital is required, for interest rate risk, for which it was not. From a bank's perspective, interest rate risk is one of many risks that it must manage to be successful.

While the problem is readily understood, the solution is not simple. Whether it is the banking agencies or banks that are evaluating interest rate risk, two separable decisions can be identified: (1) the choice of a method to measure the effects of changes in interest rates on asset, liability, and off–balance sheet values; and (2) the choice of a method to "model" the effects of such changes on the market value of a bank's portfolio or net worth. A number of measurement methods exist, the most prominent being duration, and elements of the more recently developed value at risk (VaR). A number of modeling methods also exist, including the duration-based supervisory model, other elements of VaR, worst-case scenario, stress tests like those of the OTS, yield curve twist scenarios, and Monte Carlo simulations.

Difficult issues common to all include (1) the time classifications or maturity "buckets" within which different financial assets, liabilities and off–balance sheet items can be effectively grouped; (2) the level of detail required to support such determinations; (3) the need to determine, at each individual bank, the response of bank depositors (and other creditors) to changes in market rates of interest; and (4) recognition of the dynamics of interest rate and yield curve changes.

Duration-based measures of interest rate risk are probably most frequently used; they constituted the basis for the federal agencies' 1993 proposal. Duration, however, has serious deficiencies. It becomes an increasingly worse approximation with longer-term and higher-coupon financial instruments that exhibit convexity. This is particularly the case when the convexity is negative as the result of embedded options. Even after accounting for convexity, large changes in interest rates cause a wide disparity between actual changes in market value and duration-based estimates, because duration tends to be an overly conservative measure when interest rates are rising, an insufficiently conservative measure when interest rates decline, and otherwise unrealistic for instruments with options. Duration measures need to incorporate option characteristics (e.g., of mortgage-backed securities) and valuation of interest rate options such as interest rate caps and floors (as is done by the Office of Thrift Supervision).

A key problem in all efforts to measure and model interest rate risk is interest rate volatility. There are times when, for various reasons, larger interest rate changes become more likely. During such periods, the increased volatility amounts to increased risk. In large measure, volatility is subject to considerable variation and is not predictable. Interest rate volatility hedges are available, but require contracts that are sensitive to volatility such as options on interest rates—e.g., floors, caps, options on futures, and combinations of these.

Duration and duration-based measures are impervious to risks associated with changes in interest rate volatility. When volatility increases, duration must be adjusted by imposing larger interest rate changes to shock the system. Moreover, changes in volatility are associated with twists in the yield curve. The difficulty of predicting changes in volatility undercuts the value of duration-based measures and models.

The supervisory model proposed by the federal banking agencies does include an adjustment for convexity, but may be characterized as static. Exposure is determined on the basis of a parallel shift of the yield curve by assuming a ±200 bp change in all interest rates. However, the proposed index of exposure (IRR index) behaves perversely. Similarly, the OTS model follows this methodology, but with up to a ±400 bp change in interest rates.

Further, the supervisory model accounts for neither interest rate volatility nor twists in the yield curve. It is possible to incorporate yield curve twists in a static model, but the impact, which must be identified with particular portfolios, would have to be determined on a bank-by-bank basis.

A strength of the value-at-risk approach is that it attempts to account both for interest rate volatility, through the determination of a lower limit on the likelihood of adverse interest rate changes, and for nonparallel shifts in the yield curve through the use of correlations of changes in interest rates over various maturities. However, the instability of correlations among the various interest rate changes that impact a bank's portfolio—that is, the volatility of the correlations themselves—represent another source of risk. In addition, another major drawback is that the value-at-risk approach does not properly account for both adverse increases and decreases in interest rates—volatility is not symmetrically accounted for (Kupiec and O'Brien, 1995a and 1995b).

All static measures, whatever corrections are made, are deficient because they ignore the dynamics of interest rate and yield curve changes. Empirical evidence indicates that interest rate volatility and twists of the yield curve can have a major impact on bank interest rate risk exposure. Consequently, it is necessary to develop a dynamic and stochastic model to account for volatility, the correlation of interest rates at different maturities, and their effects on a bank's value. Such a model, while admittedly more complex, offers a better approximation of reality and a more refined methodology for stress testing.

Finally, it is necessary to note that all of the models reviewed treat interest rate risk and credit risk as unrelated. This is clearly not the case. Increases in interest rates may impact bank borrowers and their expected earnings so that they cannot meet their debt obligations. On the other hand, a general decline in borrower earnings, for reasons other than interest rate changes, can lead to defaults that tend to increase interest rates and further reduce the value of a bank's equity. Further, these interactions may not be ascertainable, even in probabilistic terms. Bank borrowers may be impacted by unpredictable changes in interest rate volatility. Interest rate volatility may change abruptly as the result of unpredictable changes in business conditions and in response to Federal Reserve monetary policy, itself responding to changed business conditions.

In these circumstances, it is understandable that the integration of interest rate risk into risk-based capital requirements, as envisioned by the federal banking agencies after FDICIA was passed, has not yet been successfully accomplished. The long delay in establishing the "Final Rule" issued in August 1995, and the limited nature of the rule, reflect the complexities involved. Of particular concern are the potential side effects to any proposal, realistic or not, that may produce costs that are greater than benefits, including serious injuries to those being regulated and, in the extreme, an ineffective or perverse regulation—itself not simply being ineffective, but establishing perverse incentives and reactions by bankers.

## WHAT SHOULD BANKS AND THE AGENCIES DO?

What then, should banks and the banking agencies do? Within the current regulatory approach, it is not obvious that the answers are the same. Hedging interest rate risk seems a better approach for banks than adding to their capital. The use of swaps, for example, to hedge might be a preferred way for dealing with interest rate risk. The banking agencies, however, committed to capital requirements as the instrument of choice, may prefer additional capital to the use of derivative instruments, particularly in some cases where the behavioral characteristics of the instrument may be unclear. There may be other approaches, however, in which bank and agency objectives more nearly conform.

## The Risk Capital Approach to Capital Adequacy Determination

As discussed in Chapter 6, one approach phrases the question in terms of what is the required amount of capital necessary for bank owners to invest in order for banks to be competitive and profitable in producing these types of financial services. Equivalently, the question may be asked, What is the cost that bank owners will have to bear in order to provide the insurance on bank assets— risk management methods—necessary to permit them to be profitable and competitive? The Merton and Perold (1993, p. 17) approach that specifies this capital as "risk capital": the smallest amount necessary to insure the value of the firm's net assets against a loss in value relative to the alternative default risk-free investment of those assets. In this context, net asset value is the market value of assets less the default-free equivalent value of liabilities and other commitments.

Risk capital is, by this definition, the amount necessary to provide asset insurance so as to make liabilities default risk–free. Since liabilities are valued at their default-free value, the amount of risk capital required is independent of the capital structure of the financing of net assets. In addition, this amount of capital implies that depositors are protected and the federal deposit insurance fund is also protected.

The implication of the risk capital approach is to recognize required capital as a measure of the minimum premium to be paid for asset insurance to guarantee the payoff of liabilities at their par value at maturity.[1] Individual risk management bank practice is the method by which such insurance is provided in banking, and the concept of risk capital is an attempt to measure the minimum cost to meet the capital level required.

As previously discussed, bank supervisors have chosen bank capital as the main instrument for supervising bank risk taking. They have established a risk-based capital system to implement their policies for credit risk only. The August 1995 "Final Rule" does not impose a capital requirement and avoids making the translation from interest rate risk exposure to credit risk exposure.

Employing a concept of risk capital as the measure of the minimum cost necessary to manage risk, bank management and bank regulators can establish a single standard to measure the required costs to meet the risk needs of their customers profitably. From this measure of the cost of providing asset insurance, regulators have the information necessary to establish a capital standard to meet the risk exposure experience of the bank.

## THE FUTURE OF INTEREST RATE VOLATILITY, INTEREST RATE RISK, AND REGULATORY CONCERNS

It is not surprising that the federal banking agencies have, for the time being, at least, withdrawn the IRR index and the duration measure on which it is based as a model for determining the appropriate capital charge. This withdrawal has left the agencies with a measuring scheme (Federal Reserve Board, August 2, 1995) that, per se, has no implications for what is too much or too little risk. This is another way of saying that it has left examiners with considerable discretion.

In a sense, the agencies have already positioned themselves in a manner that more or less accords with the findings reached above. As noted, the analysis of interest rate risk is best accomplished at the individual bank level, simple formulas are not adequately realistic, and flexibility in imposing capital charges is necessary. Given the extent to which exemptions exist, it appears that capital charges may be imposed only in extreme cases. How long this situation will continue is uncertain.

It seems likely that the measurement system proposed by the agencies in their August 1995 Policy Statement is likely to be adopted sometime in the near future. Examiners will, of course, continue to evaluate the interest rate risk exposure of individual banks and may feel called upon to ask for additional capital in some cases. It is uncertain how soon the federal agencies will conclude that they have enough experience to return to a formula for converting excess interest rate risk exposure into risk-based capital requirements along the lines of their 1993 proposal, if they ever do. A formula for translating interest rate risk into risk-based capital requirements should not be expected in near future.

It seems likely, then, that for some time examiners will have considerable discretion in evaluating capital needs based on interest rate risk. If they are overly restrictive, they may compel banks to shift from interest rate risk to credit risk. If they are insufficiently restrictive, the trade-off will be in the opposite direction, with the result that the bank is undercapitalized for its risk exposure.

Whatever examiners and the agencies do, bankers must manage their risks in the most cost-efficient way possible. This implies an individualized approach to the measurement of interest rate risk, along dynamic and stochastic lines, and hedging to reduce risk; and one that encourages bank management to measure and target risk exposure consistent with the bank's resources—management, technological, and financial. In addition, bankers must be prepared to protect themselves against discretionary examiner judgments and accounting standards that may be more or less arbitrary. This also argues for an individualized evaluation system that permits a persuasive response to supervisory inquiries.

Over the longer run, the significance of interest rate risk to both banks and the federal banking agencies will depend on the movement and volatility of interest rates, and also to the evolving nature of bank operations. In discussing interest rate movements, it is useful to distinguish between long-term trends and periodic short-term disruptions.

As noted, the development of the interest rate risk problem emerged out of institutional and economic changes in the post–World War II period. Recent developments suggest that the secular increase in rates may now be over. However, with monetary policy focused on the control of inflation and employing interest rates as the principal policy instrument, rates are likely to be less volatile than in the late 1970s and early 1980s, but with the Federal Reserve as the source of volatility (e.g., the February 1994 to January 1995 period). As a result, interest rate risk, except perhaps as it applies to derivative instruments, may not be any less important than in the early 1970s, but best managed to meet the risk-return objectives and portfolio structure of the individual bank.

It is, nevertheless, to be expected that interest rate risk problems will, periodically, become acute as the result of outside events over which bankers have little or no control—for example, systemic events such as stock market declines, large financial institution failures, and monetary policy shifts. Systemic disturbances, while not predictable as to time or quantitative effect, are likely to reoccur. Monetary policy regimes, which have shifted abruptly in the past, can shift abruptly again.

## FINAL COMMENTS

The need to develop capital regulations for interest rate risk for commercial banks became a logical necessity in a risk-based capital environment; moreover, the absence of capital requirements for some kinds of risk would seem to create incentives to trade off one kind of risk, for which capital had been required, against another risk, for which it was not.

A capital charge for interest rate risk is, in itself, not sufficient to prevent trade-off incentives. Even if a capital charge is imposed, the trade-off could be in either direction, depending on relative costs. This is likely because neither credit risk weights nor estimates of interest rate risk exposure are likely to accord with market realities and in the same way for each bank. The problem could be alleviated by the exercise of discretion by examiners, but it could also be exacerbated.

Despite the underlying relationships between interest rate and credit risk, they are, in important ways, noncomparable from a bank's point of view. Once the federal banking agencies establish more or less stable risk weights for various types of credit, a bank can, through its portfolio management policies, decide how much capital is optimal. If the risk weights are realistic, bank decisions will efficiently reflect profit opportunities. With respect to interest rate risk, the capital amounts required by a realistic evaluation can shift abruptly as interest rate volatility shifts, possibly as the result of outside events. Incremental capital amounts cannot be established by a bank within a time frame appropriate for asset-liability management. A regulatory effort to establish capital requirements in this fashion can periodically confront banks with unexpected and high costs.

It follows that capital requirements may be a useful instrument for both the agencies and banks in the case of credit risk; there is no other effective way to hedge credit risk under the current system in which diversification is not given appropriate consideration.

But capital requirements are not likely to be the optimal instrument for banks in managing their interest rate risk; there are other ways to hedge.

The federal agencies' approach (and the related approach of the Basle Committee) do not, as yet, provide a meaningful operational design for measuring and modeling interest rate risk, either to assess capital or for bank risk management. If the agencies eventually do impose a more formal system, something like their September 1993 proposal, including an explicit formula for translating interest rate risk into credit risk for purposes of capital assessment, it is likely to fall more heavily on some banks than on others. As a result, the system is likely to be injurious to competitive performance of individual institutions, and to competition between the banking industry and unregulated financial institutions. Even if the type of model proposed by the agencies is never adopted, elements of it could be imposed in a discretionary manner in the course of the examinations process.

Banks, of course, need to manage their interest rate risk independently of regulatory requirements. They require a systematic reporting system for interest rate risk, just as they need other types of cost accounting systems. It would be useful if the systems they adopt can be used for their own management purposes and for reporting to the agencies. They also require a probabilistic model for determining effects of measured interest rate risk on the value of bank equity.

Banks are now more accustomed to dealing with interest rate risk than they were when the problem was relatively new. Different banks appear to be moving in different directions. Some large organizations are, apparently, shortening their asset maturities considerably. At the same time, they may be taking substantial interest rate and/or credit risk in their off–balance sheet activities. Others are heavily invested in longer-term securities. It seems clear that interest rate risk, as it is incurred and managed, will continue to differ from bank to bank. Like other aspects of FDICIA, the effort to constrain discretion and substitute relatively rigid rules can be, at best, only partially successful.

In this regard, we find ourselves in agreement with Chairman Greenspan's statement cited above:

> . . . technological advances breed increasing numbers of ways to take on risk as well as increasing numbers of ways to measure and control

risk. . . . No single quantitative standard or ratio could capture this diversity across institutions, nor even capture the complexity of risk at any one institution . . . ; regulatory formulas may, in fact, stifle productive innovation.

To which we would append the perceptive comment of Walter Wriston on the current regulatory *zeitgeist*: "Capital adequacy has become a race with no finish line."[2]

## NOTES

1. See Chapter 6 for valuing the premium and specifying it as a put option on the net asset value of the bank. The volatility specification would include the volatility of interest rate changes as well as credit risk and foreign exchange risk.
2. The statement is from an op-ed essay entitled "Bank Weaknesses Are a Regulatory Illusion" that appeared in *The Wall Street Journal* on February 7, 1992.

## REFERENCES

Black, Fisher, and Myron Scholes. "The Pricing of Options and Corporate Liabilities, *Journal of Political Economy* 81 (May–June 1993), pp. 637–54.

Federal Reserve Board, Press Release, *Interagency Advance Notice of Proposed Rulemaking to Revise Risk-Based Capital Standards,* July 30, 1992.

Federal Reserve Board, "Press Release on 'Prompt Corrective Action',"
September 18, 1992.

Federal Reserve Board, Press Release, *Interagency Notice of Proposed Rulemaking to Revise Risk-Based Capital Standards,* September 14, 1993.

Federal Reserve Board, "Press Release Regarding the Basle Committee on Banking Supervision Proposal for Incorporating Market Risk, April 12, 1995.

Federal Reserve Board, Joint Agency Policy Statement: Supervisory Policy Concerning a Supervisory Framework for Measuring Credit and Assessing Banks' Interest Rate Risk. Exposures, Washington, D.C. August 2, 1995.

Kupiec, Paul H., and James M. O'Brien (1995a). "Internal Affairs," *Risk* 8, no. 5 (May 1995), pp. 18–20.

Kupiec, Paul H., and James M. O'Brien (1995b). "A Pre-Commitment Approach to Capital Requirements for Market Risk, draft, Board of Governors of the Federal Reserve System, April 1995.

Merton, Robert C. "An Analytical Derivation of the Cost of Deposit Insurance and Loan Guarantees: An Application of Modern Option Pricing Theory, *Journal of Banking and Finance* 1 (June 1977), pp. 3–11.

Merton, Robert C., and André F. Perold. "Theory of Risk Capital in Financial Firms" Continental Bank *Journal of Applied Corporate Finance* 6 (Fall 1993), pp. 16–32.

Wriston, Walter B. "Bank Weaknesses Are a Regulatory Illusion," *The Wall Street Journal*, February 7, 1992.

# Index

Thank you for choosing Irwin Professional Publishing for your business information needs. If you are part of a corporation, professional association, or government agency, consider our newest option: Irwin Professional Custom Publishing. This allows you to create customized books, manuals, and other materials from your organization's resources, selected chapters of our books, or both.

Irwin Professional Publishing books are also excellent resources for training/ educational programs, premiums, and incentives. For information on volume discounts or Custom Publishing, call 1-800-634-3966.

Other books of interest to you from Irwin Professional Publishing . . .

### THE TREASURER'S HANDBOOK OF FINANCIAL MANAGEMENT
*Applying the Theories, Concepts and Quantitative Methods of Corporate Finance*
Treasury Management Association

Treasury management encompasses a board spectrum of corporate finance—from capital structure and working capital management to capital budgeting and risk management. Whether the treasury manager oversees one or many apsects of the company's finances or outsources them, this book is a critical tool to be used for understanding and managing short and long-term financial issues.
ISBN: 1-55738-884-9                    500 pages

### INTEREST RATE SPREADS AND MARKET ANALYSIS
*Tools for Managing and Reducing Rate Exposure in Global Markets, Seventh Edition*
Citicorp

Although there has not been, and may never be, a formula to predict the future movement of interest rates and market volatility, financial managers must still contend with the pressures of investing and financing amidst global market uncertainty. *Interest Rate Spreads and Market Analysis* is designed to foster an understanding of key global market rates and prices, providing a 10-year historical database for long-term short-term indices.
ISBN: 1-55738-862-8                    300 pages

### MANAGING FINANCIAL RISK
*A Guide to Derivative Products, Financial Engineering and Value Maximization*
Charles W. Smithson with Clifford W. Smith, Jr. & Wilford D. Sykes

Provides a system for evaluating a varied continuum of financial risks, and offers techniques and strategies for maximizing the value of a firm in the face of risk. Includes an in-depth evaluation of various risk management products, including forwards, futures, swaps, options, and hybrid securities—as well as a "building block" approach to implementing these products in your firm.
ISBN: 0-7863-0008-6                    600 pages

## PROTECTING SHAREHOLDER VALUE
*A Guide to Managing Financial Risk*
Abraham M. George

Protecting Shareholder Value discusses the risks that shareholders face from exposure of their companies to foreign exchange and interest rate changes. It also discusses how management can effectively deal with the uncertainties in financial markets to protect the value of the firm.
ISBN: 0-7863-0439-1                    500 pages

## INTEREST RATE RISK MANAGEMENT
*The Banker's Guide to Using Futures, Options, Swaps and Other Derivative Instruments*
Benton E. Gup & Robert Brooks

As banks invest more and more in mortgage-based securities and other interest-sensitive products, their exposure to interest rate risk increases proportionately. Now *Interest Rate Risk Management* tackles this important issue, presenting simplified, non-technical examples of how to use derivative securities to protect against swings in interest rates, explaining why some interest rates are more volatile than others, and demonstrating how to use derivative securities effectively in any financial services business.
ISBN: 1-5573-8370-7                    275 pages